FACTORY RECORDS
THE COMPLETE GRAPHIC ALBUM

FAC 461

FACTORY RECORDS
THE COMPLETE GRAPHIC ALBUM

MATTHEW ROBERTSON

CHRONICLE BOOKS
SAN FRANCISCO

FAC 461

CONTENTS

Fac 0 — Factory Catalogue No.
X — Page

1978	Fac 1 **18**	Fac 3 **19**	Fac 4 **19**	Fac 2 **20**	**1979**	Fac 5 **21**	Fac 6 **22**	Fact 10 **23**	Fac 13 **24**	Fac 11 **24**	Fac 12 **25**	Fac 7 **25**
Fact 14 **26**	Fact 16c **27**	**1980**	Fac 13 **24**	Fac 23 **28**	Fac 23 **28**	Fac 21 **28**	Fact 25 **29**	Fac 18 **30**	Fac 18 **30**	Fact 30 **31**	Fact 17 **31**	Fac 22 **32**
Factus 2 **33**	**1981**	Fact 24 **33**	Fac 33 **34**	Fac 33 **34**	Fac 33 **35**	Fac 39 **36**	Fac 29 **38**	Fac 31 **38**	Fac 19 **38**	Fac 34 **38**	Fact 35 **39**	Fac 32 **39**
Fbn 8 **39**	Fac 49 **39**	Fact 45 **40**	Fac 47 **42**	Fac 53 **43**	Fact 40 **44**	Fact 50 **45**	Fact 44 **46**	Fac 52 **46**	Fac 48 **46**	**1982**	Fac 66 **46**	Fact 55 **47**
Fac 59 **47**	Fac 43 **47**	Fac 63 **48**	Fac 63 **48**	Fac 41 **49**	Fac 51 **50**	Fact 65 **54**	Fac 62 **58**	Fac 57 **58**	Fac 58 **59**	Fac 67 **60**	Fact 60 **60**	Fact 70 **60**
Fbn 21 **60**	Factus 8 **61**	Fact 37 **61**	Fact 56 **61**	**1983**	Fac 73 **62**	Fac 83 **63**	Fact 75 **64**	Fac 64 **66**	Fac 68 **66**	Fbn 23 **67**	Fac 72 **67**	Fac 82 **67**
Fac 79 **67**	Fac 93 **68**	Fact 74 **69**	Fac 78 **70**	Fbn 24 **70**	Fact 71 **71**	Fact 77 **71**	Fact 89 **71**	Fac 81 **71**	**1984**	Fac 88 **74**	Fac 97 **74**	Fac 102 **74**
Fact 90 **75**	Fac 120 **76**	Facus 21 **77**	Xmas 84 **78**	Fac 126 **78**	Fac 103 **79**	Fbn 22 **79**	Fac 111 **80**	Fact 95 **80**	Fbn 34 **80**	Fac 96 **80**	Fac 107 **80**	Fac 106 **80**
Fact 84 **81**	Fact 80 **82**	Fact 85 **84**	Fac 112 **85**	**1985**	Fac 114 **86**	Fac 119 **86**	Fac 122 **86**	Fac 113 **86**	Fbn 41 **87**	Fac 116 **87**	Fac 117 **87**	Fac 124 **87**
Fact 100 **88**	Fac 51 3rd b'day **90**	Fac 123 **91**	Fbn 36 **92**	Fac 128 **93**	Fbn 46 **94**	Fact 144 **95**	Fac 129 **96**	Fact 110 **97**	Fac 145 **97**	Fac 127 **98**	Fac 138 **98**	Fact 130 **98**
Fac 134 **98**	Fact 135 **99**	Fac 147 **99**	Fact 155 **99**	**1986**	Fac 143 **100**	Fac 139 **103**	Fact 140 **103**	Fac 51 4th b'day **104**	Fac 142 **105**	Fac 151 **106**	Fac 151 **108**	Fac 151 **109**

Fact 150 **110**	Fac 153 **110**	Fac 163 **110**	Fact 166 **113**	Fac 168 **113**	Fac 158 **114**	Fact 165 **114**	Fac 162 **114**	Fac 51 D Mach **116**	Fact 164 **117**	**1987**	Fac 86 **72**	Fac 141 **103**
Fac 179 **114**	Fac 176 **115**	Fac 167 **116**	Fac 146 **116**	Fac 187 **116**	Fact 170 **119**	Fac 157 **120**	Fac 203 **121**	Fac 51 5th b'day **121**	Fac 183 **122**	Fac 183R **123**	Fact 200 **124**	Fac 184 **126**
Fact 190 **126**	Fac 169 **126**	Fac 188 **126**	Fac 196 **127**	Fac 178 **127**	Fact 185 **127**	Fac 192 **127**	Fac 197 **128**	Fac 193 **129**	Fac 214 **131**	Fact 204 **131**	**1988**	Fac 240 **130**
Fac 194 **132**	Facd 224 **132**	Fac 73R **133**	Fac 198 **134**	Fact 205 **134**	Fact 160 **134**	Fact 195 **134**	Fact 206 **134**	Fac 51 6th b'day **135**	Fac 51 6th b'day **135**	Fac 213 **136**	Fact 250 **139**	Fac 212 **140**
Fact 220 **144**	Fac 223 **147**	Fac 223 **147**	Fac 223R **147**	Fac 235 **149**	**1989**	Fact 275 **148**	Fac 263R **150**	Fac 263 **150**	Fac 263DJ **150**	Fac 263 **151**	Fact 244 **152**	Fact 244 **153**
Fact 260 **154**	Fact 217 **154**	Fac 222 **155**	Fac 51 7th b'day **156**	Facd 219 **157**	Fac 231 **157**	Fac 229 **157**	Fac 201 **159**	Fac 201 **163**	Fac 273 **164**	Facd 276 **165**	Fact 236 **166**	Fact 226 **167**
Fact 246 **167**	Fact 256 **167**	Fact 266 **167**	Fac 232 **168**	Fac 228 **169**	Fac 242 **170**	Fac 242R **171**	Fac 247 **172**	Fac 257R **172**	Fac 257 **173**	Fac 245 **174**	Fac 51 Flowers **174**	Fac 281 **174**
1990	Fac 221 **175**	Fac 51 8th b'day **176**	Fac 269 **177**	Fact 249 **177**	Fac 258 **177**	Fac 268 **178**	Fac 272 **179**	Fac 278 **179**	Fac 298 **179**	Fac 302 **179**	Fac 51 USH **180**	Fac 293 **181**
Fac 293R **181**	Fac 251 **182**	Fac 251 **183**	Fac 311 **185**	Fact 230 **186**	Fac 267 **186**	Fact 274 **187**	Fact 320 **188**	Fac 295 **190**	**1991**	Fact 290 **191**	Facd 316 **192**	Facd 326 **192**
Facd 336 **192**	Facd 346 **192**	Facd 356 **193**	Fac 284 **194**	Fac 287 **195**	Fac 287 **195**	Fac 287R **195**	Fac 312 **196**	Fac 312R **196**	Fac 51 Halluç. **197**	Fac 297 **198**	Fact 285 **198**	Fact 310 **199**
Fac 308 **199**	Fac 51 9th b'day **200**	Fact 210 **201**	Fact 325 **201**	Fac 307 **202**	Fac 319 **202**	Fact 337 **202**	Fac 329 **202**	Fact 322 **203**	O2 Logo **204**	Fact 314 **206**	Fact 324 **206**	Fact 334 **206**
Fact 344 **206**	Fact 400 **207**	Fac 332 **208**	Fac 328 **210**	**1992**	Fac 51 10th b'day **211**	Fac 201 3rd b'day **212**	Fac 351 **212**	Fac 327 **213**	Facd 366 **213**	Facd 406 **213**	Fact 335 **214**	Fac 347 **214**
Fac 362 **215**	Fact 420 **216**	Fac 372 **217**										

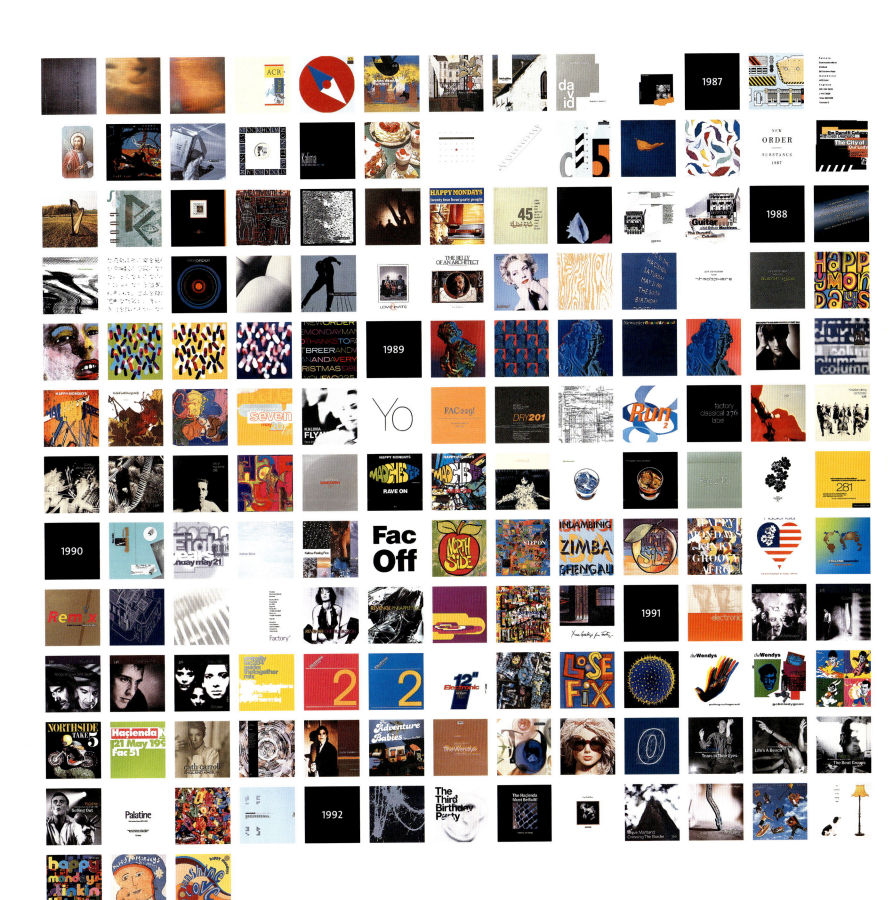

DE QUOI T'OCCUPES TU EXACTEMENT ?
DE LA RÉIFICATION
NON, JE ME PROMÈNE. PRINCIPALEMENT JE ME PROMÈNE.

1978: year zero for Factory, and Britain was still in the dark ages, at least as far as design was concerned. Despite the joy of Psychedelia in the sixties, the post-war fifties had not been swept away, merely swept under the carpet to emerge again in the drab corporatist early seventies.

I like to think that this book shows a new, colourful, exactly drawn dawn in those dark days. I recall a phone call one night a few years ago from one of the central figures in this book, the 'man in dressing gown', the legendary Peter Saville. Peter had rung to discuss an exhibition at the Festival Hall in London; I think it was called 'Destroy' and was supposed to be an exhibition of Punk artwork, posters, sleeves and drawings delightfully sandwiched in plastic. I had been surprised when the organizers had asked for some of our stuff ('our' being Factory) since we were post-Punk and would not flatter ourselves with the four-letter designation. Peter had rung to say he'd just been to the exhibition. Which had closed. So he'd missed it.

No surprise there. But he had heard one of the curators talking on Radio Four, explaining that it was these posters and record sleeves for a bunch of avant-garde bands who emerged in the wake of the Pistols, that had kick-started what became known, laughably, as 'Designer Britain'. The D.B. tag may be reviled today, yet how unbearable if we still had to live in a country where that revolution had never happened. How much better to dress in black than in grey, metaphorically speaking.

It all began after a very, very bad Patti Smith gig in late '77 or early '78 at the Manchester Apollo; as I was leaving I was stopped by a young man (he probably looked like Bryan Ferry on a good day after a bad night – that's the way he always looks) who said he was a graphic designer and if I ever needed some work doing he was the man. Two weeks later he came to see me and we sat in the Granada canteen. Did he bring some work to show me? Yes. Was it his work? No. It was a book on Jan Tschichold. I was hooked. We pored over covers for Hoffman-LaRoche catalogues and Constructivist posters and Penguin book covers. I am obsessed with people who are cleverer than me. Peter was cleverer than me.

Two months later I'm sitting cross-legged on the floor of a flat in Hale while this kid moves blocks of black and yellow around on the floor. A general contemplating his troop formations. That was Fac 1. I suggested that our first record should be Fac 1, but Peter objected. 'No, that was the poster, this has to be Fac 2.' And since it was a double 7-inch single – the first I could remember since *Magical Mystery Tour* – the appropriateness of the Factory numbering system was born. By chance. Like everything else.

It was a fantastic idea to differentiate our little cottage industry record label (run out of Alan Erasmus and Charles Sturridge's flat in a Manchester suburb) by having sleeves that were glossier, more expensive and more beautiful than those of the multinationals. Great

idea, only we never had it. We just did what we wanted to do. And then post-rationalized it. We clothed our singles in glossy sixties-EP-style packages. And then men like the great and sadly late Scott Piering, Rough Trade plugger extraordinaire, would stand outside Radio One pulling the indie vinyl out of its glossy arty sleeve and inserting it into a white nondescript 7-inch bag, to make it look as if it came from a major label.

Why was packaging important for us? Because the job was a sacred one. Music had transformed our young lives, children of the sixties all. And now we were in the privileged position of putting out records ourselves. Does the Catholic Church pour its wine into mouldy earthenware pots? I think not.

We started with hand made, to get the finish we wanted, from stuffing the silver paper of Fac 2 into plastic bags to paying Joy Division to glue sheets of sandpaper – Naylor's Abrasives, Bredbury – to the Durutti Column album (Alan shouldn't have brought in the porn video, as the guitarist, drummer and bassist watched the vid and left their singer to do the gluing – semen-like paste everybloodywhere, like something out of Erasure). By the way, the picture of Fact 14 hides the fact that after the sleeves dried, they hardened into curves and valleys which made the surface even more destructive.

Although Factory's heritage seems to be one of perfect design and typography, that is no more than half the story. Tim Booth of James came in one day with the artwork for his first single. He presented us with a seven inch square of green felt-tip hurriedly wiped across white paper. 'OK, you want something like this?'. 'No. I want this.' 'OK.' Tim thought he was epataying the bourgeoisie. In fact we thought it was a great idea to completely go against the grain and have a piece of undesigned rubbish. It was about time.

While Saville may have designed the definitive acid house sleeve with *Fine Time*, the second half of the Factory story is best summed up by the painterly eccentricity of Central Station, of Matt, Pat and Karen. That cover of *Bummed*, the outside a black-and-white photo covered with oil paint, the inside that got ten thousand copies returned by US distributors and upset Genesis P. Orridge (yes, I'll repeat that, it upset Genesis P. Orridge). It wasn't the fact the woman was middle aged, it wasn't the shaved pubes, it was the colour quality which made the viewer feel dirty. Sheer genius, that.

And so it goes for all those who created the images in this book. Thinking about it all brings to mind wonderful memories; wonderful memories of wonderful people with whom I and my partners were privileged to work. Exasperated, but privileged.

Factory was more than just a label – it was a cultural institution. Not only did it produce some of the most acclaimed records of the period – including the output of Joy Division, New Order and the Happy Mondays, to name only three bands – but it also gave rise to some of the most stimulating artwork and design of the late 20th century. Today, while Factory may have ceased to exist as a commercial entity, its spirit and influence endure in popular culture mythology, and its unique and chaotic story has been revisited again and again, in magazine articles, television documentaries, music compilations and the 2002 feature film *Twenty-Four Hour Party People*. Without doubt one of the factors in this longevity has been the label's emphasis on design. Over a fourteen-year period, between 1978 and 1992, Factory created and sustained a visual profile admired and emulated worldwide, one that placed it alongside the labels Blue Note, ECM and 4AD as an archetype of the successful marriage of music and design. Even though each label thought carefully about the appropriate design approach, only Factory had a multi-faceted programme that took design to the core of its being. Indeed, it is fair to say that Factory pushed design further than any record label, past or present. Its non-conformist vision gave rise to some of the most innovative sleeves of the era and led the company into ambitious and era-defining three-dimensional projects, setting it apart still further from its contemporaries.

From the beginning Factory was more of a collective of like-minded individuals than a structured business – profitability was always a secondary concern. This freewheeling approach to the business of running a record label, whereby the rules were made up as they went along, probably meant that Factory was destined to disintegrate from the outset. In many ways, it is a wonder that it lasted as long as it did. Its unconventional approach extended to not signing contracts with artists and avoiding promotional duties; co-founder Tony Wilson, originally a Granada TV presenter, saw Factory as 'a laboratory experiment in popular art'. Its survival was propped up by the success of its major acts Joy Division, New Order and the Happy Mondays.

The catalyst behind the formation of Factory was the Punk movement of the 1970s. This cultural rebellion sought to break down barriers and give everybody the opportunity to participate in intellectual and/or aesthetic production on their own terms, irrespective of any formal 'talent' or 'skill'. Untrained musicians were empowered to form bands, while untrained designers could produce the artwork. While Punk had a strong collective aesthetic, the defining characteristic (and most important lesson) of the age was this DIY – do-it-yourself – ethos.

Factory's direct link to Punk can be traced to an evening in June 1976, when Wilson and actor Alan Erasmus attended a performance by the Sex Pistols at the Lesser Free Trade Hall in Manchester. Fired up by this spirit Wilson and Erasmus established a club night showcasing the new generation of bands inspired by the same movement. Their action was in part entrepreneurial, in terms of creating a space for this burgeoning scene, but they were also genuinely passionate music enthusiasts themselves. There remains a difference in opinion as to how Factory was chosen as a name for this club night, but the usually accepted version is that Erasmus came up with it in recognition of a parallel between industrial creativity that takes place in a factory and musical creativity. The name is inextricably linked to Manchester's post-industrial sense of place, while at the same time drawing on Pop artist Andy Warhol's notions of collective creativity in a 'factory' environment.

These sentiments, and the notion of independence, had particular resonance given Factory's base outside London, the music industry capital (just as much today as in the late 1970s). As in most regional centres, the staunch local pride found in Manchester fostered a culture of self-reliance. The same sense of self-containment and community could be found among creative circles, whereby musicians, promoters, venues, recording studios, retail outlets and designers were all constituted into a localized network. Factory, a product of this mini-system, found more than enough talent within it to sustain the label.

From the outset Factory demonstrated a commitment to design. Not only did it commission a young graphic designer, Peter Saville, to create the poster for the opening night of the club (see p. 18), but it also made him a partner alongside Wilson and Erasmus. Saville would go on to define the label's visual programme and educate his associates in the process. Wilson concedes that it was unlikely that Factory would have pursued such a design programme had Saville not been involved. The poster was given the label's first catalogue number, Fac 1, beginning a tradition that would last to the very end (and beyond).

In September 1979 Joy Division's manager Rob Gretton become the fifth partner in Factory, alongside Wilson, Erasmus, Saville and record producer Martin Hannett. They found not only an ally, but also someone who shared as much passion for music and creativity. Gretton's similar disregard for mainstream values bolstered the Factory spirit and over the years allowed the band's success to feed back into the label. This generosity facilitated many of the label's whims, supported younger bands and sanctioned Peter Saville's free hand in designing Joy Division's (and New Order's) artwork. Gretton, who passed away in 1999, played a pivotal role in the Factory story.

For most record labels, design means little more than the obligatory packaging – a means to an end. Although they invest time and money in the construction of seductive branding, it is ultimately mere styling. Rarely is there the volition to push things further, let alone to make design central to the label. Factory, however, believed that its products had real significance and that there was a critical relationship between the manufacturer and the consumer. Although the word Factory carries with it connotations of faceless mass-production, there was something boutique and considered about its products. On this point, Wilson has said that Factory aimed to create a form of communication between the label, the creator of artifacts, and the people who buy the artifacts. He has also said that the relationship between Factory and its public was based on mutual respect and a desire to produce the most beautiful objects imaginable.

Factory's body of work offers us myriad designed visions. This grand design narrative is woven together by Factory's unique take on the indexing systems normally used for stock management. Factory designated catalogue numbers to practically everything it was involved in, from recorded releases to posters, stationery (see p. 25), a nightclub (Fac 51: The Haçienda – see p. 50), an outlet for Factory ephemera (see p. 174), and even a civil lawsuit brought against them by a disgruntled business partner. This meant that all items allocated a number were not only branded as Factory products, but were given greater currency by placing them within a specific cultural context.

Peter Saville, Tony Wilson and Alan Erasmus / 1979

Factory Logo / 1979 / Des: Peter Saville

Fac 2 Various Artists *A Factory Sample* / Double 7-inch / 1978 / Des: Peter Saville

Factory took every available opportunity to make their items unique beginning with the first record release, Fac 2. This double 7-inch, designed to emulate records from the Far East with a plastic-wrapped gatefold sleeve, was unconventional without being flamboyant. All 5,000 copies were sold, setting the label on its way. There are countless examples of the label producing such distinctive items, even going so far as to commission different artwork for 7- and 12-inch formats, not to mention fully designed covers for 12-inch remixes at a time when most remixes were released in perfunctory white sleeves.

This total approach to design extended to three built projects: The Haçienda (Fac 51), Dry bar (Fac 201) and Factory HQ (Fac 251). Upon the completion of the latter Wilson claimed to have successfully triangulated the city of Manchester with buildings in the north, south and west. These projects, all designed by Ben Kelly, gave a physical dimension to the language and aesthetic of Factory. Both The Haçienda and Dry were radical statements that set new standards for club and bar culture in Britain. The sensibilities and attitudes activated these spaces, yet neither was in any way kitsch. These proved to be the label's most costly ventures.

From the outset, Factory played with a set of visual codes that would act as a beacon for the like-minded, and possibly as an active deterrent for the uninitiated general public. For the very first commission – Fac 1, the poster advertising a series of club nights at the Russel Club – Peter Saville set about combining the modernist typography of Jan Tschichold with industrial warning iconography sourced from his college to create what he describes as 'urban utilitarianism'. By avoiding more obvious promotional techniques, Saville allowed the audience to come up with their own associations, and this remained the defining methodology running through Factory's design. Although Saville and other designers progressed from this early industrial aesthetic, it acted as a default setting for the label.

Factory's codified language, signified by minimal information and an emphasis on the index number, would quickly become a graphically recognizable style. The frequent absence of 'necessary' data would give the label a unique visual identity that distanced it from its contemporaries. This approach acknowledges that the consumer is visually receptive, fosters a brand loyalty that does not rely on usual marketing manipulation, and celebrates the sleeve as a legitimate space for communication. This approach was especially evident in the Joy Division and New Order sleeves.

Fac 51 The Haçienda / Nightclub / 1982 / Des: Ben Kelly Design

Commenting on this design approach, *New York Times* journalist Jon Pareles went so far as to suggest that it was akin to some big secret. In reviewing New Order's 1989 album *Technique*, Pareles wrote that the album 'continues New Order's long-established marketing mystique. It's packaged with a minimum of information. But the band members' names, faces and instrument credits are still absent, as are lyrics; song titles are related to the songs obliquely, if at all. The lack of data makes every fan an initiate, sharing a mass-produced secret'. Factory's refusal to promote bands in the established manner, which included avoiding interviews, only contributed to this mythology.

This approach was perhaps most obvious in The Haçienda. This space shunned all the commonplace devices one would expect of a nightclub in the early 1980s. Instead of a luminous neon sign outside, Kelly specified a small engraved granite panel discreetly set into the building's brick exterior. Once inside the club, it was designed as a journey of discovery with clues left along the way – a theatre-like space, where everyone could play a role. The Factory experience offered the public an opportunity to engage with design in a totally new way.

Indeed, Factory design was an aesthetic education for a generation. Through sleeves, ephemera and built spaces, devotees of the label were inculcated into the nuances of design language. In albums especially, the imagery had a resonance that would have been less potent in other circumstances. Saville talks about a 'hearts and minds' theory, the proposition that design was able to cross over into the consciousness of a new generation via popular music. The music inspired a more direct passionate and physical response, while the design suggested a lasting cerebral dimension. Certainly Factory was responsible for dozens of indelible images that many individuals have carried into later life.

Factory's preoccupation with design also attracted a degree of suspicion and criticism. By establishing a brand and presenting itself as an acutely style-conscious organization, the label flew in the face of the anti-establishment sentiment of independent music, and led some to claim that it was all style over substance. Writer and journalist Jon Savage wrote in *The Face* that despite Saville's impressive work, his design for Section 25 was 'an object exercise in over-design, and a clear indication that the designer has become more important than the group'. Others, meanwhile, saw the industrial aesthetic as pretentious, oppressive and cold. Morrissey, lead singer of The Smiths, took flowers on stage at The Haçienda as a protest against its clinical atmosphere. Although Factory was very much connected to Manchester's historic past, it could be argued that it romanticized the working-class reality of the factory floor. Saville himself has reflected that the appropriation and use of this industrial language bordered on conceit, given his middle-class, pastoral upbringing. And the warehouse design of The Haçienda was not that far removed from the working environments of many of the club goers.

While Peter Saville may have laid the foundations of the Factory style, he did not by any means design everything for the label. His departure to London in 1979, combined with increasing fees, lack of interest in certain briefs and a tendency to deliver rather slowly, soon opened the doors for other aspiring designers (though he would keep a firm grip on the representation of New Order and higher profile projects). It also presented the opportunity for non-

Fact 10+4 Poster / 1979 / Des: Peter Saville

designers to take responsibility for producing artwork. Bands including The Wake, ACR, Swamp Children, and even Tony Wilson himself, had a hand in the design side of things.

Given the strong sense of community in Manchester, and the cult following that Factory had already built up in a short space of time, it was not hard to find new design talent, even within the music scene. With this came a range of approaches. Some of these new designers worked in accordance with the de facto house style set by Saville, but others took the opportunity to experiment. New relationships formed between bands and designers, ones which in most cases were mutually beneficial. It is fascinating to trace the evolution of individual designers and observe their development relative to the band. Many designers practising today launched their careers at Factory.

After Saville, the most prolific of the thirty or so designers commissioned by the label were Martyn Atkins, Mark Farrow, Trevor Johnson (later in partnership as Johnson Panas), 8vo and Central Station Design. Their distinctive approaches diversified the Factory lexicon, with each individual body of work demonstrating a visual journey of discovery, from elementary exercises to sophisticated compositions. This rich assortment of varied practices is itself a microcosm of the design industry.

Martyn Atkins was one of the first independent designers to take on work for Factory after Saville. Atkins had worked with Saville on several projects including Joy Division's album *Closer* (see p. 29). His own output was a deviation from the austere nature of this work, injecting a degree of graphic wit. The 12-inch design for Fac 18 – Section 25's *Girls Don't Count* (see p. 30) – is the antithesis of the 7-inch version designed by Ben Kelly and Peter Saville. Instead of industrial vernacular the viewer is presented with suburban kitsch. Atkins would go on to design artwork for other eighties bands including Depeche Mode and Echo and the Bunnymen, before finally becoming a photographer and film director based in California.

Peter Saville / 1984   Central Station Design / 1989

In 1982 Mark Farrow, a local graphic designer inspired by Saville's work, was commissioned to design the 7-inch single for new Factory act Stockholm Monsters. He made his own exuberant statement using mock-leather paper stock and foil stamp printing (see p. 49). Over a series of sleeves Farrow's work challenged given formats and production techniques, with varying results (though also winning him several prestigious design awards). By the 1990s he had become one of the most renowned sleeve designers around, having defined the graphic profile of the Pet Shop Boys and worked with other performers such as the Manic Street Preachers, Kylie Minogue and Spiritualized.

Trevor Johnson's debut was also unusual, an LP cover that worked both independently and as part of a larger composition when combined with eight other copies of the album (see pp. 82–3). Johnson's highly competent appropriation of 20th-century graphic motifs, iconography and lettering would be a key attribute of his early work. By 1986 Johnson would be in partnership with Tony Panas, and as Johnson Panas they would become key designers of the Manchester scene. Johnson has continued to generate a phenomenal amount of work, playing a key role in the visual landscape of contemporary Manchester.

8vo were established in 1984 by designers Mark Holt and Michael Johnston, with Hamish Muir joining the following year. Holt, who had previously worked for the label, was approached to design The Durutti Column's fourth LP for Factory (see p. 81). Confident in their methodologies, 8vo reacted against the broader design language of Britain at the time, and demonstrated greater interest in typographically led communication. They recall Wilson's usual brief being 'Just make it better than the last time!', and saw such open briefs as an opportunity to experiment, drawing parallels between their own practice and the progressive nature of The Durutti Column's music. Other significant works include their five poster designs for The Haçienda nightclub anniversaries between 1985 and 1991. Their body of work is a prime example of the evolution of practice and is also an example of designers making the transition from analogue to digital production methods with the arrival of desktop publishing in the late 1980s. Their output, including their self-published typographic journal *Octavo*, would have a major impact on British design in the following years, leading to consultancy work for major organizations including American Express and Thames Water.

The boldest rejection of the Factory style actually came from within the label through the work of Central Station Design. The work produced by brothers Matt and Pat Carroll and Karen Jackson is the antithesis of the Saville look. Loose, humorous, playful, layered, multi-coloured constructs confounded those who recognized the label for its austere, minimal and at times self-referential output. Central have frequently expressed their disdain for the almost elitist attitude of many designers, and as much as they respected Saville, imitation was never on the agenda, since they could only design in a way that reflected their own experiences. In any case the music scene in Manchester had changed dramatically since the late 1970s. The close relationship between their work and the music they designed for is primarily down to the fact that the Carroll brothers were close relatives of Shaun Ryder and Paul Ryder, respectively singer and bass player in the Happy Mondays. Shortly after their formation, the Mondays were caught up in one of the biggest pop cultural periods in the UK since Punk. The rave and 'Madchester' scenes brought together electronic dance music from the US with a home-grown brand of guitar-based rock; and this fusion also coincided with the arrival of the drug Ecstasy from the continent. Central Station's day-glo palette coloured that scene, and features prominently in the Factory catalogue from 1988 onwards, infiltrating the work of most of the other designers. In the same way that Saville branded the post-Punk movement, so too did Central brand the rave generation.

Upon its move in 1990 to new premises in Manchester's Charles Street (known as Fac 251 – see p. 183), Factory employed, for the first time, a full-time designer to deal with the considerable workload. Shortly before the move, Saville's design firm, Peter Saville Associates (PSA) had designed the new Factory logo and a formal style guide for the application of brand marks across all products. Things had clearly changed from the early days, and many designers looked back with nostalgia to the younger, more carefree Factory. With the shadow of bankruptcy looming large, for the first time marketing decisions played a role in the design and promotion of goods. Until these final days, Factory's designers enjoyed a freedom rarely seen in commissioned visual practice, effectively being given the same creative license that the musicians enjoyed. All those involved celebrate the fact that Factory never provided a brief in commissioning projects, the creative engine instead being the band or the designer. Even Ben Kelly in designing The Haçienda was never given a formal brief, just a budget. And while freedom of creativity can conjure its own problems (Saville is brutal in his proposition that designers are often 'messengers who help other people how to say things ... don't give an open brief as they have no idea what to do, cause they do not have anything to say'), by and large the designers who worked for Factory did have something to say. Sometimes this was an artistic or political statement, but just as often it was a comment on design itself.

Factory's output can be seen as embodying what the late designer Dan Friedman called a 'culture of optimism'. In his book *Radical Modernism*,

Fac 83 *Haçienda 1 Year* posters in situ / 1983   Fac 251 *Factory HQ* prior to refurbishment / 1988

Friedman proposed that some of the most inspirational design came from periods when designers allowed 'fantasy to supersede functionalism'. There were many instances when humour, fantasy, play and personal expression could drive the design process. Factory itself was an eternally optimistic proposition, given its own fragility, which gave designers the opportunity to follow their vision. Saville admits that the label gave him the chance to create the world that he wanted to see. Humour pervades the story, from the attitudes of the founders to the sleeves of Martyn Atkins and Central Station Design, and even in naming the downstairs bar in The Haçienda 'The Gay Traitor' in reference to Anthony Blunt, the art historian and KGB Cambridge spy. Although there was an unequivocal commitment to the project at hand, nothing was taken too seriously.

Factory's legacy today exists on many levels. The success and redevelopment of modern-day Manchester owes a huge debt to Factory, yet with offshoots in the Benelux countries, America and Australia, the label was also a global brand. Not only did it have some of the most innovative bands and interesting approaches to design, but arguably the world's most famous nightclub, The Haçienda. Opened in a converted yacht showroom, it set new standards in club design, and had a global impact on club culture (as well as making Manchester a beacon of acid house). Fac 201 Dry was also a remarkable addition to Manchester's nightlife and was way ahead of its time in terms of bringing a Barcelona-standard bar to provincial Britain. Factory's effective reactivation of decayed urban spaces is now the norm, despite being unheard of at the time, and bars like Dry are scattered throughout the city. In the same vein, loft apartments, Tony Wilson's unfulfilled dream envisaged in 1984 (Fac 101), are now the standard for inner-city living. These interventions helped redefine the fabric of this modern city.

Similarly Factory's legacy continues to influence the creative industries to this day, whether as a literal appropriation of the label's obvious graphic signifiers, or in the adoption of the more minimal visual codes used by the label. But this is not surprising given that the creative decision-makers of today grew up during the post-Punk era. More importantly, Factory brought design to those less likely to be exposed to it in everyday life, through record sleeves, ephemera and built spaces. These strategies were not calculated manoeuvres designed to exploit the consumer – rather, they were about aspiration, making something more of our lives. Compared to the hijacking of design by marketing and advertising, this is a case study of a real alternative space to thrive. In a consumer culture that increasingly diminishes our desire to create, Factory continues to inspire a range of individuals in their pursuits including design.

My first encounter with Factory was when my older sister brought home a copy of Fac 143 *Shellshock* (see pp. 100–101). It felt like it had come from another world, offering no image of the band. It was not until much later I actually saw a photograph of New Order that swiftly dissolved the imaginary portrait in my mind – much like seeing a radio deejay for first time. By the time I was in my late teens, the Happy Mondays, riding the 'Madchester' wave, also captured my imagination thanks largely to their artwork. I remember producing my own versions of *Pills 'N' Thrills...* using local sweet wrappers. And my classmate's self-censored copy of *Bummed* with underwear added in black marker to avoid the stir it would cause in his conservative household. This story is not unique and many fans across the world could testify to similar experiences. So it is not surprising to meet many other designers who attribute their chosen profession to the label (despite Peter Saville's belief that Factory actually misled a generation into believing that all designers have unlimited freedom).

This book, Fac 461, is the first attempt to capture the visual output of Factory. Initially the thought was to arrange the work by Fac number, but since the attribution of the catalogue numbers became more and more erratic – for example, New Order singles always had to end in a '3', while important projects always ended in '1'– instead the work appears in more or less chronological order. The few non-design items in the Fac catalogue (for example, Rob Gretton's dental bill – Fac 99) are listed at the back, to appease completists. And in most cases vinyl versions of artwork have been illustrated since they show the design off better than CD or cassette-tape versions. Finally, at times the book strays outside the Fac catalogue – for example, with the Haçienda flyers – or else delves into the catalogues of Factory offshoots such as Ikon, Factory Benelux and Factory US. In this way, hopefully I have been able to tell the full story of this remarkable label.

Following spread:
Fact 75 New Order *Power, Corruption & Lies* (detail) / LP / 1983 / Des: PSA

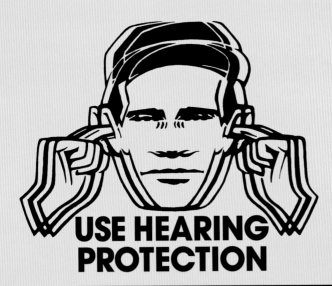

USE HEARING PROTECTION

MAY 19-THE DURUTTI COLUMN/JILTED JOHN

MAY 26-BIG IN JAPAN/MANICURED NOISE

THE FACTORY

JUNE 2-THE DURUTTI COLUMN/CABARET VOLTAIRE

JUNE 9-THE TILLER BOYS/JOY DIVISION

RUSSEL CLUB ROYCE RD MOSS SIDE

Fac 1 The Factory Club No. 1 / Poster / 1978 / Des: Peter Saville

Fac 1, the poster opposite, marks the beginning of the Factory catalogue. Appropriating diverse sources including the typographic characteristics of Jan Tschichold's *Die Neue Typographie* (1928), the colour scheme of the UK's National Car Parks, and a warning sign from Saville's college workshop, it was designed to advertise the first four nights of the Factory club. Though it was delivered after the debut event, and only earned Saville £20, the poster laid the foundations of Factory's design programme. The next two promotional posters (Fac 3 and 4, below) again quote Tschichold, but from his later classical period. Co-founder Tony Wilson claims that he designed Fac 4 , though Saville is resolute in his authorship.

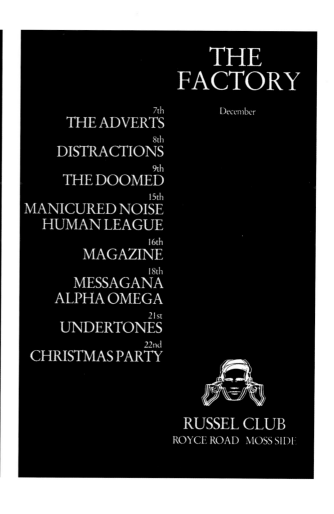

THE FACTORY

Friday October 20th

JOY DIVISION

CABARET VOLTAIRE

THE TILLER BOYS

RUSSEL CLUB
ROYCE ROAD
MOSS SIDE

THE
FACTORY

7th
THE ADVERTS
8th
DISTRACTIONS
9th
THE DOOMED
15th
MANICURED NOISE
HUMAN LEAGUE
16th
MAGAZINE
18th
MESSAGANA
ALPHA OMEGA
21st
UNDERTONES
22nd
CHRISTMAS PARTY

December

RUSSEL CLUB
ROYCE ROAD   MOSS SIDE

Fac 3 *The Factory Club No. 2* / Poster / 1978 / Des: Peter Saville   **Fac 4** *The Factory Club No. 3* / Poster / 1978 / Des: Peter Saville

Factory's first recorded release was a double 7-inch EP featuring Joy Division, The Durutti Column, John Dowie and Cabaret Voltaire. Having explored other graphic directions (see p. 19), Saville returned to the language of the original Fac 1 poster, with the central motif being sourced and redrawn from a leaflet on industrial standards. Tony Wilson suggested the plastic-sealed gatefold format, which was inspired by record packaging found in the Far East. The single came with a set of four stickers that represented each of the bands showcased on the release. Printed in silver and black in an edition of 5,000, it was clear from the outset that Factory sought to create objects that went far beyond normal expectations.

FAC-2

A FACTORY SAMPLE

Fac 2 Various Artists *A Factory Sample* / Double 7-inch / 1978 / Des: Peter Saville

A Certain Ratio gave Peter Saville a selection of images for the band's first single, including the 1966 photograph of controversial American comedian and satirist Lenny Bruce found dead from a drug overdose. Members of the band were fans of Bruce and felt that the image was suitable for the sleeve in terms of his lifestyle and the violent subtext of the song. The subject matter, and various technical limitations, led Saville to design a sleeve based on Andy Warhol's 1960s *Death and Disaster* series, in which horrific images were used as a statement on the desensitizing effects of violence in the media. The other side of the sleeve, as well as the record label itself (see below) featured another of the band's selections, an image of actor Anthony Perkins in Alfred Hitchcock's 1960 classic, *Psycho*.

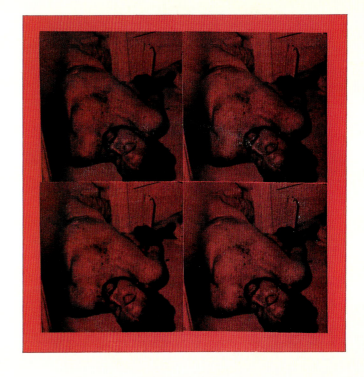

A Certain Ratio *All Night Party*

Detail from *Fac 5,* 1979
Paper and vinyl construction in an edition of 5000
Produced by Martin Zero at Cargo Studios, Rochdale

45 rpm, a Factory Product

G & L

Fac 5 A Certain Ratio *All Night Party* / 7-inch / 1979 / Des: Peter Saville

Shortly before designing this sleeve, Peter Saville discovered a book on alternative systems of graphic notation in 20th-century avant-garde music. Since the members of OMD also used their own abstracted handwritten marks to score music, Saville took a set of their notations and used dry-transfer lettering to render them as precise marks. The composition and type choice is again inspired by Jan Tschichold's later period, while the artwork is printed in black thermographic ink, to emulate braille, on similar-coloured card stock – a reference to the 'Dark' in the band's name.

Fac 6 OMD *Electricity* / 7-inch / 1979 / Des: Peter Saville

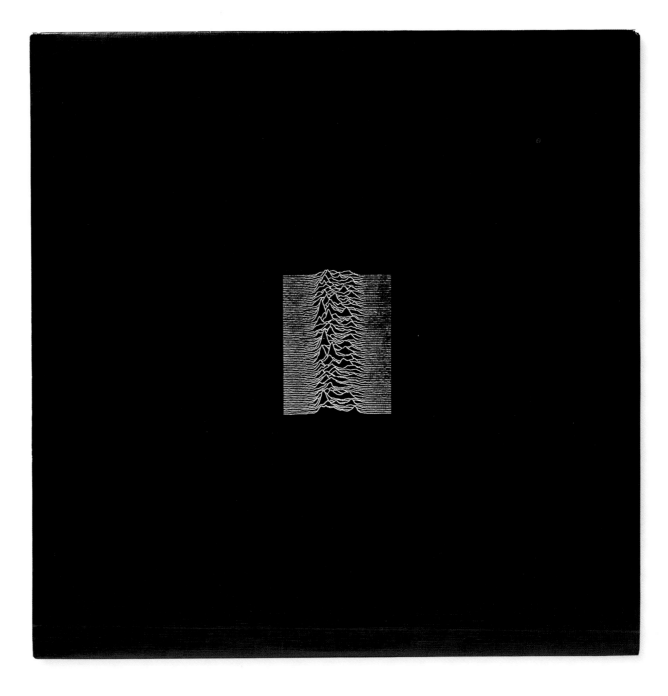

Unknown Pleasures, Joy Division's first LP, has one of the most iconic album covers of the post-Punk era, with the spatial dynamics, otherworldliness and vulnerability complementing the music perfectly. As with Fac 5, the band supplied Peter Saville with an image: in this case a diagrammatic representation of the first pulsar discovered, CP 1919, which became the focus of the sleeve. Sourced from page 111 of the *Cambridge Encyclopaedia of Astronomy*, it represents the radio waves emitted from a collapsed star. Saville shows an acute sensibility to form through his handling of the image – the diagram is not overstated, but instead floats in deep space, with all typographic information put on the back cover. Long-playing releases were designated by the prefix 'Fact' within the catalogue.

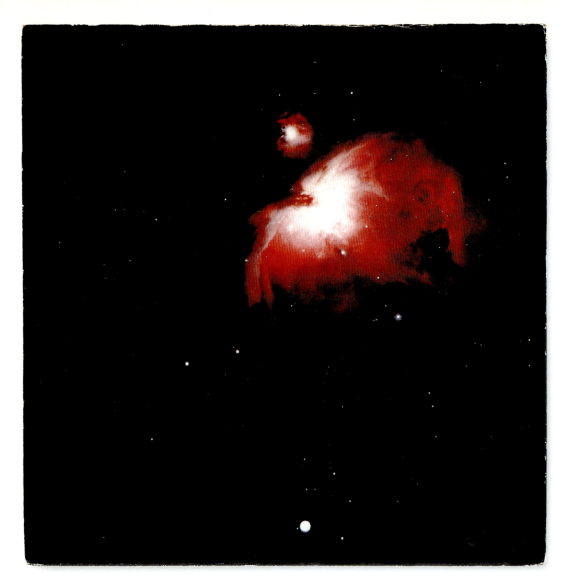

Fac 13 Joy Division *Transmission* / 12-inch / 1980 / Des: Peter Saville

The artwork for Joy Division's first 7-inch single, a photograph of deep space, is a logical progression from the representation of *Unknown Pleasures*. There is the suggestion of ethereality – 'the possible source of the message' alluded to in the song's title, according to Saville. The sleeve for the 12-inch version (above), designed months later, does not implicitly relate to the preceding artwork, though the images of an amusement park at night again play with light and dark — from the cosmos to the fairground.

Fac 13 Joy Division *Transmission* / 7-inch / 1979 / Des: Peter Saville

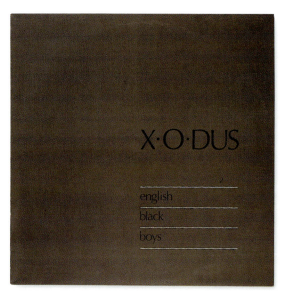

Fac 11 X-O-Dus *English Black Boys* / 12-inch / 1979 / Des: Peter Saville

THE DIS TRA CTI ONS

TIME GOES BY SO SLOW

Fac 12 The Distractions *Time Goes By So Slow* / 7-inch / 1979 / Des: Peter Saville

FAC 7

The first Factory logo is a visual pun on production graphs, each rectangular bar representing a different value. Peter Saville was simply toying with the concept of industrial productivity. This logo appears on the first set of stationery (right), as well as on several recorded releases (right, above). The label allocated Fac numbers to each set of stationery it commissioned over the next thirteen years (see Fac 141, p. 103, and Fac 311, p. 185).

FACTORY RECORDS
86 Palatine Road, Manchester 20.
Telephone 061-434 3876

Fac 7 Factory Notepaper / Stationery / 1979 / Des: Peter Saville

Early on Factory drew a great deal of influence from the Situationist International, a revolutionary political and artistic movement founded in the 1950s by Guy-Ernest Debord (see also p. 8). In 1959 Debord, with the help of artist Asger Jorn, produced *Mémoires*, a book bound in raw sandpaper designed to damage all other publications around it. Durutti Column member Dave Rowbotham was inspired by the concept and suggested it to the rest of the band. This was the embodiment of Punk agitation – a radical gesture through a simple DIY act. Record stores complained that the sleeve had damaged other stock, but paradoxically the music itself is delicate and cerebral, and far from aggressive.

Fact 14 The Durutti Column *The Return of The Durutti Column* / LP / 1979 / Des: Dave Rowbotham

The PVC packaging for ACR's first cassette-only LP is designed as a clutch bag or strapless purse, in reference to the word 'ballroom' in the title. The cases were made by an importer of thermoplastic bags who Saville had befriended soon after his move to London in 1979, and came in several different colours, including green and orange, with slight variations in the packaging design. The cassette label features Saville's logo for the band, 'a✓:', with the tick denoting certain and the colon ratio. The front image of four men was taken from the cover of a knitting pattern.

Fact 16c A Certain Ratio *The Graveyard and the Ballroom* / Cassette / 1979 / Des: Peter Saville

This cover is an adaptation of designer Ben Kelly's 1974 thesis for the Royal College of Art, which was engraved with the title *Metal Lined Cubicles* and Kelly's pseudonym 'The Photo Kid'. Saville saw the hard material as suggestive of the contemporary urban spirit he wanted to capture, and so with photographer Trevor Key set about recreating the oxidized steel form. However, given the melancholic nature of the song, and Curtis's suicide very soon after recording the track, many fans read the final artwork as a headstone. The cover took on an iconic significance beyond its intended purpose.

Fac 23 Joy Division *Love Will Tear Us Apart* / 7-inch / 1980 / Des: Peter Saville / Ph: Trevor Key

Fac 23 Joy Division *Love Will Tear Us Apart* / 12-inch / 1980 / Des: Peter Saville / Ph: Bernard-Pierre Wolff

Martyn Atkins originally designed this as a possible new Factory logotype. Based on the 'f'-hole cut into string instruments (such as a violin), its elegance was a far cry from the industrial aesthetic of the label at that time. However, before it got as far as Factory, Peter Saville thought it would be suitable for Fractured Music, Joy Division's company. The mark was applied to several of the band's releases and has often been mistaken for a Factory signifier.

Fac 21 Fractured Music / Logotype / 1980 / Des: Martyn Atkins

,CLOSER,

Fact 25 Joy Division *Closer* / LP / 1980 / Des: Martyn Atkins & Peter Saville / Ph: Bernard-Pierre Wolff

The now-iconic image on the cover of *Closer* is a photograph by French photographer Bernard-Pierre Wolff. Taken in 1978, at the Staglieno Cemetery in Genoa, it shows a crypt filled with figures in mourning. This Neo-Classicist imagery was complemented with typography based on a 2nd-century Roman alphabet. These elements combine with the textured stock to create a visual experience that mirrors and enhances the music. The imagery of the cover took on greater significance after the suicide of lead singer Ian Curtis, which happened during the manufacturing of the album. Although the concept for the sleeve had been approved by the band before his death, both the label and designers were accused of exploiting the tragedy when it was decided not to withdraw the artwork.

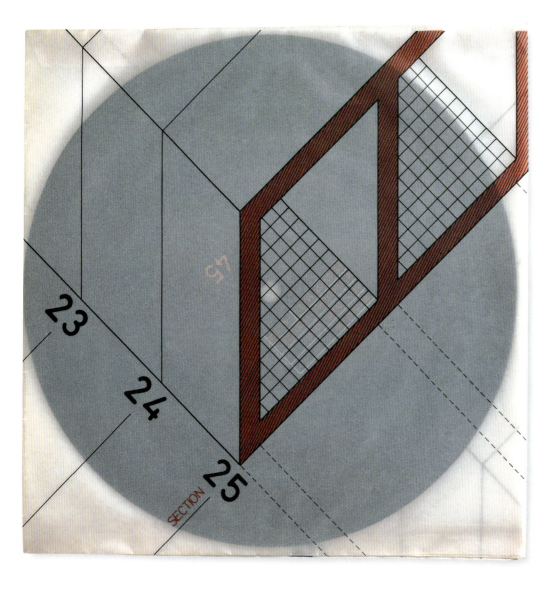

Fac 18 (left), designed in collaboration between Ben Kelly and Peter Saville, is a response to the name of the band, Section 25, as opposed to any specific reference to the music. An axonometric detail, printed on semi-transparent paper, employs the graphic language of architecture and industrial planning. This technical aesthetic perpetuates the already existing utilitarian codes of the label, while the transparent paper stock offers a tactile multi-layered experience and shows Factory's usual willingness to work with unconventional materials.

Fac 18 Section 25 *Girls Don't Count* / 7-inch / 1980 / Des: Ben Kelly & Peter Saville

Fac 18 Section 25 *Girls Don't Count* / 12-inch / 1980 / Des: Martyn Atkins

The 12-inch version of the sleeve shows a radically different approach to that of the 7-inch. The band gave designer Martyn Atkins photographs of their girlfriends and sister to appear on the sleeve, a departure from the usual music industry practice of playing down the female companions of male performers. Atkins proposed three different sleeves, one with each portrait, and intentionally set about making a humorous statement by combining the low-grade images with a gaudy typeface and specifying a gloss-laminated stock – all very much at odds with the Factory 'look' up to that point.

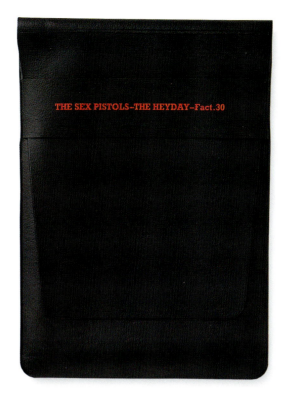

Fact 30 The Sex Pistols *The Heyday* / Cassette / 1980 / Des: Peter Saville

Fac 17 Crawling Chaos *Sex Machine* / 7-inch / 1980 / Des: Jon Savage

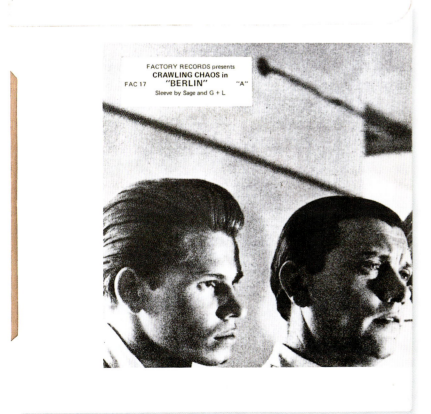
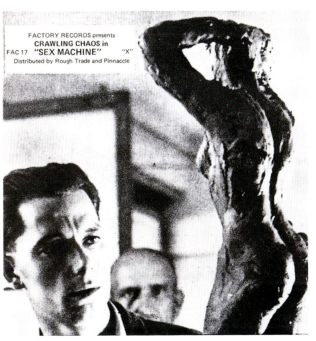

A Certain Ratio *Blown Away*
Detail from *Fac 22*, 1980
Produced by Martin Hannett at Revolution Studios, Cheadle and Strawberry Studios, Stockport
45rpm, a Factory Product

ACR commissioned their friend Ann Quigley, later of Swamp Children and Kalima, to make a painting for the single *Flight*. Quigley came up with the image of an angel on a bed. Meanwhile, Tony Wilson, the band's manager at the time, commissioned a set of studio portraits of the group: photographed without shirts and with stylized haircuts, this projection stood in contrast to the shrouded mystique of label mates Joy Division. These photos, along with the painting and a set of woodblock prints, were handed over to Peter Saville and Martyn Atkins to create the sleeve design: the designers had no direct correspondence with the band and fashioned the 12-inch single on the preceding Fac 5 (see p. 21).

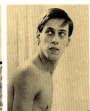

A Certain Ratio *Flight. And then Again*
Detail from *Fac 22*, 1980
Written by A Certain Ratio and published by the Movement of the 24th January Publishing
45rpm, a Factory Product

Fac 22 A Certain Ratio *Flight* / 12-inch / 1980 / Des: Peter Saville & Martyn Atkins /
Ph: Daniel Meadows / Painting: Ann Quigley

Factus 2 Joy Division *She's Lost Control* / 12-inch / 1980 / Des: Peter Saville / Ph: Charles Meecham

JOY DIVISION

FACT 24 – 'A Factory Quartet'

Side One – The Durutti Column
Side Two – Kevin Hewick

Side Three – Blurt
Side Four – The Royal Family and the Poor

Fact 24 Various Artists *A Factory Quartet* / Double LP / 1981 / Des & Ph: Tony Wilson

Factory frequently demonstrated its openness to design in allowing the designer to create different artwork for the 7-inch and 12-inch versions. The smaller version of *Ceremony* (left) was designed to resemble an ecclesiastical inscription in reference to the title of the song. The original 12-inch version (opposite), meanwhile, used the Albertus type specimen designed by Berthold Wolpe in 1937, to emulate a ceremonial banner. According to Saville this was one of the first stages of his 'grand tour for the masses' – a visual journey of cultural heritage through popularized media. The designer was given the opportunity to revise the artwork when it was reissued months later. The new, white version with the vertical blue bar was based on the camera-ready artwork of the previous version. The blue strip was an overlay to indicate the area to be printed as red on the original – a happy accident of sorts.

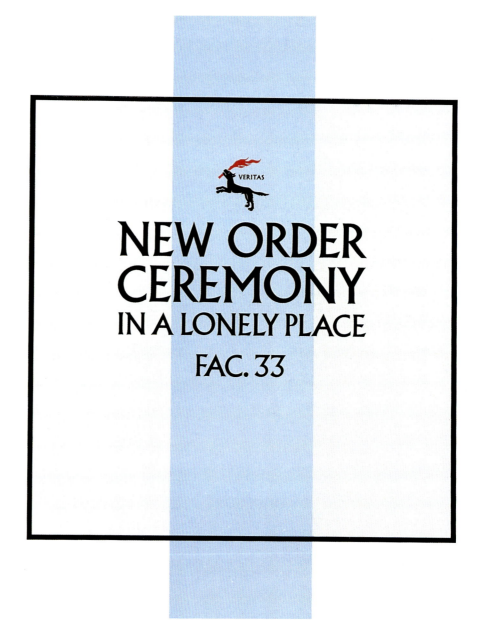

Fac 33 New Order Ceremony / 7-inch / 1981 / Des: Peter Saville & Brett Wickens
Fac 33 New Order Ceremony (reissue) / 12-inch / 1981 / Des: Peter Saville & Brett Wickens

**NEW ORDER
CEREMONY**
IN A LONELY PLACE

FAC. 33

Fac 33 New Order *Ceremony* / 12-inch / 1981 / Des: Peter Saville & Brett Wickens

watching [*woching*] *i* observe, be a spectator of;
keep under close observation; guard carefully;
note carefully; keep vigil, stay deliberately awake;
be alert; be on the look-out; w. for await alertly;
w. out be on one's guard; w. over guard, protect
~ watch *n* observation, act of watching; alertness,
vigilance; vigil; small timepiece worn or carried
on the person; (*naut*) period of duty on deck; (*ær*)
man or men employed to preserve public order.

the [*THi/THe*] *def art* indicating a particular person,
thing, class etc; used before certain titles; used
before adjectives to make them nouns; (*coll*) my;
[*THee*] (*coll*) unique; outstanding, excellent;
fashionable ~ the *adv* by that amount; to that
extent.

hydroplanes [*hi*dROplayn] *n* motor-boat designed
to skim over the surface of the water; board fixed
to motor-boat enabling it to skim; seaplane;
rudder controlling vertical movement of sub-
marine.

39

Watching the Hydroplanes is an example of a sleeve produced without any consultation whatsoever between the band and designer. The designer knew little about the band and in turn perpetuated a degree of intrigue around their identity. Inspired by unusual phrases such as 'tunnel vision' and 'hydroplanes', Martyn Atkins set about rendering all the information as dictionary definitions. However the composition, colours and choice of materials are all designed to stimulate interest and create an object that is enticing.

tunnel [tunel] n underground passage, esp one cut for a railway or road to pass under a hill, river etc; burrow ~ tunnel (pres/part tunnelling, p/t and p/part tunnelled) v/t and i dig a tunnel (through).

vision [vizhon] n act or power of seeing, sight > PDP; that which is seen; range of sight; something seen in a dream, prophetic trance, mystical experience etc; imaginative wisdom, esp concerning the future; foresight, insight; description of the future.

on [on] prep above and touching; covering; supported by; at the date of; on to; concerning; near to; (coll) at the expense of; to the loss of ~ on adv in contact; in position; continuing uninterruptedly or in the same direction; functioning, yielding power, heat, motion etc; taking or about to take place, not cancelled; (coll) willing; at stake; o. and off now and then, intermittently; o. and o. without interruption ~ on adj (cricket) to left of the batsman ~ on n (cricket) on-side.

factory [fakteRi] n building in which goods are manufactured; trading-post in foreign country; F. Acts Acts of Parliament controlling working conditions in factories.

39

These sleeves illustrate the range of work being produced both by designers and by the bands themselves. Martyn Atkins's work features predominantly here. His sleeve for Fac 31 is an appropriation of the Philips corporate brand, combined with images of a food mixer supplied by the band. Fac 19 is a visual pun on the song title *It's Hard to Be an Egg* using white vinyl with a feather stuck to the plastic sleeve. For Fact 35 ACR got Ann Quigley again (see p.32) to do a painting for the front cover with Peter Christopherson, former Hipnosis designer and member of Throbbing Gristle, to coordinate the artwork. The hands playing the trumpet are based on those of Jazz musician Miles Davis. Quigley also took responsibility for the artwork of her own band Swamp Children, while New Order had a hand in the design of their own artwork for the Factory Benelux release *Everything's Gone Green* in 1981.

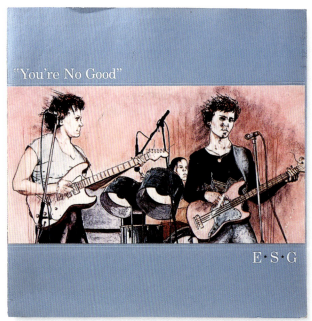

Fac 29 The Names *Night Shift* / 7-inch / 1981 / Des: Ian Wright
Fac 31 Minny Pops *Dolphin Spurt* / 7-inch / 1981 / Des: Martyn Atkins / Ph: Minny Pops

Fac 19 John Dowie *It's Hard to Be an Egg* / 7-inch / 1981 / Des: Martyn Atkins
Fac 34 E.S.G. *You're No Good* / 7-inch / 1981 / Des: Stephen Horsfall

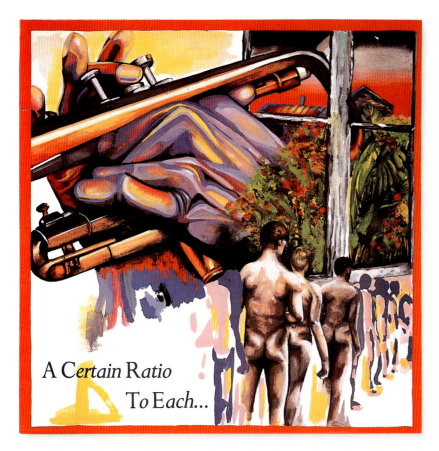

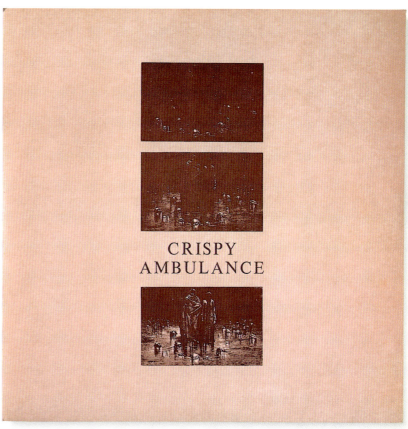

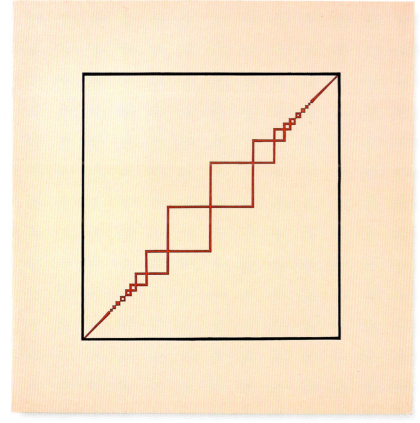

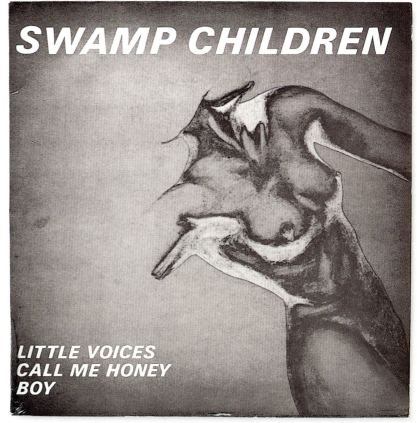

Fact 35 A Certain Ratio *To Each...* / LP / 1981 / Des: Peter Christopherson / Painting: Ann Quigley
Fbn 8 New Order *Everything's Gone Green* / 12-inch / 1981 / Des: New Order

Fac 32 Crispy Ambulance *Unsightly & Serene* / 10-inch / 1981 / Des: Martyn Atkins
Fac 49 Swamp Children *Little Voices* / 12-inch / 1981 / Des: Ann Quigley

Always Now would be one of the most overly elaborate sleeves in the entire Factory catalogue. Designed as an envelope, lined with marbled paper, and housed within a further sleeve, it was described by Jon Savage as an 'object exercise in over-design'. According to Saville the sleeve is a juxtaposition of the European and the Oriental, the first being represented by the Bembo typeface, classical typography, and psychedelic marble paper, the latter represented by the red seal on the reverse. This unorthodox combination of approaches and materials came in response to the freedom the designers had and the confidence that came with this.

45 fact | Always now | Sect 25

Section 25–Always now friend ly fires dirty disco c.p. loose tal k costs lives inside out melt clos e hit babies in the bardo be bra ve new horizon produced by martin hannett engineer joh n caffrey recorded at brittania row disegnatori : grafica indu stria e typografica berthold a factory records product fact 45

16.5 mm (60p)   10   20

Fact 45 Section 25 *Always Now* / LP / 1981 / Des: Peter Saville & Grafica Industria

Section 25

DESIGN : GRAFICA INDUSTRIA
MARBLED PAPER N° 938
REPRODUCTION AUTORISEE PAR
LA STE. KELLER - DORIAN
PAPIERS. F R A N C E

FACTORY
COMMUNI
CATIONS
LIMITED

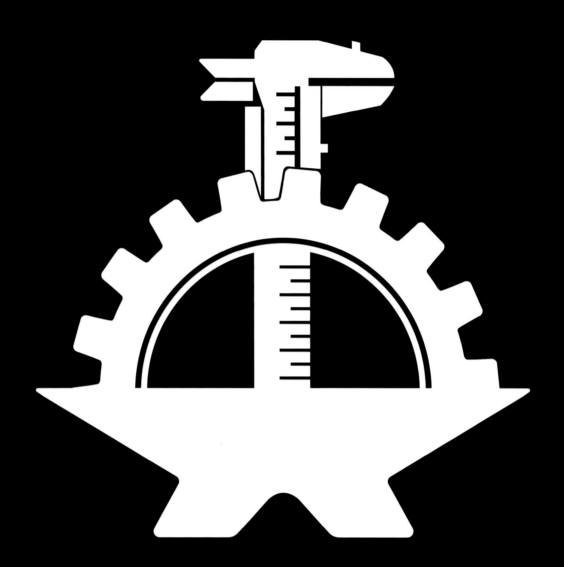

In November 1980 the label officially became a limited company trading as Factory Communications Ltd. It transpired that the name Factory Records had already been registered by an unrelated party. Saville was commissioned to design the company's logo, which he sourced from an Italian printing book. The monogram perpetuated the label's romance of industry. However, the most serendipitous aspect to this was that once the logo was flipped the letters f, c and l appear, 'F' being the vice, 'C' the cog (rotated 90 degrees), and 'L' defined by vertical axis and right hand of the anvil.

Fac 47 *Factory Anvil* / Logo / 1981 / Des: Peter Saville

Saville's interest in Italian graphics is further demonstrated here in
the sleeves of New Order's second single. Based on Futurist Fortunato
Depero's *Dynamo* (1927), it came in nine different colour versions, specified
by different band members, their management and the designers. This
decision in turn made the singles desirable as a collectible set. The sleeve
features no typographic information other than a catalogue number '53'
on the reverse. The original source material for this single and the album
Fact 50 (see p. 45) were both chosen by the band after Saville showed them
a book on the subject.

In 1982 Factory issued a compilation of previously unreleased Joy Division material. The sleeve was made from a recycled stock, though it was also available in a heavy board cover, bound by a silk sash. This release was designed as a dignified conclusion to the band, whose remaining members had gone on to form New Order. The austere cover, with block-printed lettering in Copperplate, has a simplicity that aims at longevity – the eternal.

Fact 40 Joy Division *Still* / Double LP / 1981 / Des: Grafica Industria

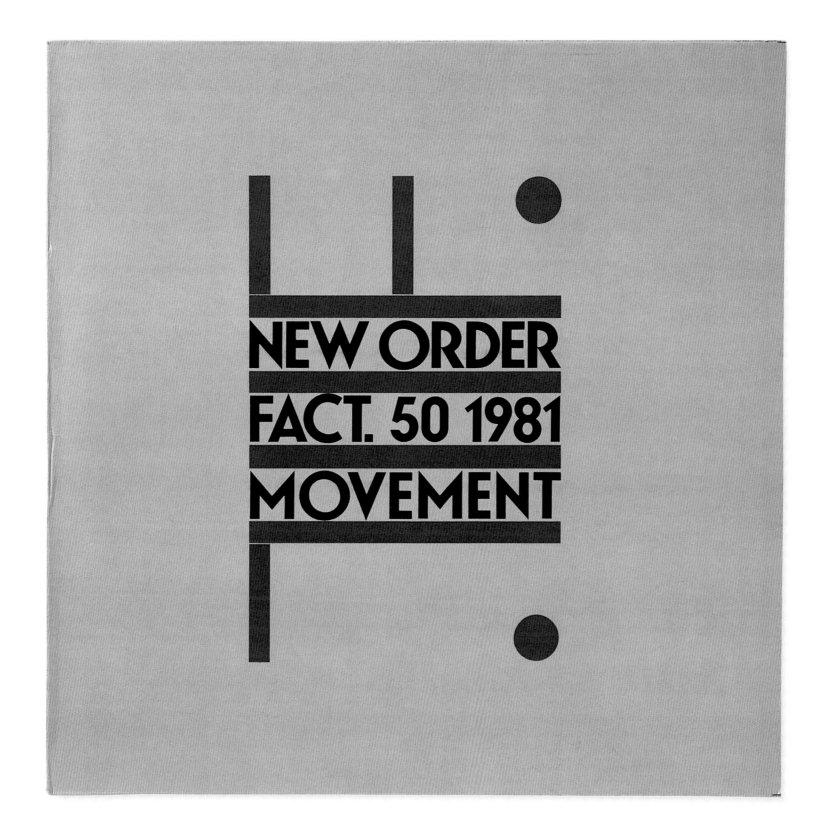

Movement is based on Fortunato Depero's cover of the *Futurismo* journal of 1932. The designers made subtle changes by substituting the text and reconfiguring the graphical elements. The F and L shapes respectively stand for 'Factory' and the catalogue number '50' in roman numerals. The band had received criticism for the choice of their name and its Fascist connotations, and although there was no such agenda to the band, the Italian Futurist references only fuelled the fires of controversy since the movement was closely aligned with right-wing politics. Saville claims that New Order's management were aware of this and requested that he remove the credit that directly identified the source of the original artwork.

Fact 44 The Durutti Column *LC* / LP / 1981 / Des: Les Thompson / Painting: Jackie Williams

Fac 52 A Certain Ratio *Waterline* / 12-inch / 1981 / Des: Ben Kelly / Painting: Denis Ryan

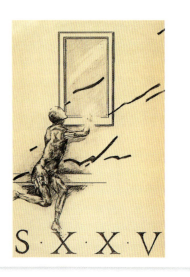

Fac 48 Kevin Hewick *Ophelia's Drinking Song* / 7-inch / 1981 / Des: Martyn Atkins
Fac 66 Section 25 *The Beast* / 12-inch / 1982 / Des: Mark Farrow

Fact 55 A Certain Ratio *Sextet* / LP / 1982 / Des: Ben Kelly / Painting: Denis Ryan

The image on this sleeve is a detail of a sunset taken from a religious painting sourced by members of ACR and chosen solely for its colours. This was handed over to designer Ben Kelly who combined it with a typeface, Bernhard Cursive, he found in Roland Penrose's *The Road is Wider than Long*. The key image for this also appears at a reduced size on Fac 52 (see opposite).

Fac 59 52nd Street *Look Into My Eyes* / 12-inch / 1982 / Des: Uncredited
Fac 43 Royal Family & The Poor *Art Dream Dominion* / 12-inch / 1982 / Des: Uncredited / Drawing: Arthur McDonald

This is one of the only sleeves by Saville that makes a direct reference to the lyrics of a song, which in this case includes the words green, blue and grey. These images were created by blowing paint, to conjure the effect of a colourfield painting. Continuing the restriction of typographic content, the 7-inch version (right) is purely abstract, while the 12-inch has text embossed on white stock.

Fac 63 New Order *Temptation* / 7-inch & 12-inch / 1982 / Des: Peter Saville & Brett Wickens

Mark Farrow, like several young designers in Manchester at the time, was drawn to Factory's unique atmosphere and keen to make his mark. In reference to the song title, he sourced a paper stock that simulated leather grain and specified all text to be foil blocked to emulate the binding of an antiquarian book. Printed in two different colours, green and burgundy, Farrow's ambitious design was not cheap to produce but certainly established his career as a designer for the label. Work like this was done in his own time after hours in the studio he was employed in. Farrow remembers the day job being boring and living for music graphics.

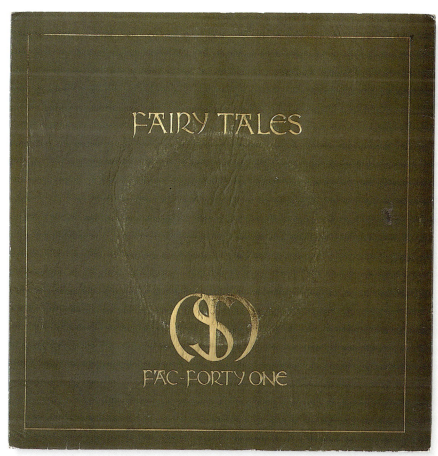

FAC51 THE HAÇIENDA

In May 1982 Factory Records, in partnership with the band New Order, opened its own nightclub in a semi-derelict area in the centre of Manchester. Drawing inspiration from various New York clubs, and taking its name from a Situationist text, Ivan Chtcheglov's 1953 essay 'Formulary for a New Urbanism', The Haçienda became one of the most iconic club spaces in the world. The club's mythology came about not only through its association with the band and label but also through its radical design, by Ben Kelly. Upon the recommendation of Peter Saville, Kelly was commissioned to redefine the former yacht warehouse into a multi-purpose space that could function as a club, bar or venue. In response he created a stark industrial interior that would become the quintessential definition of the Factory aesthetic. Clubgoers would journey through an assemblage of materials and motifs as far from a traditional British nightclub at that time as could be imagined. From the galvanized shutter entrance, to a dance floor demarcated with bollards and hazard stripes, it was a physical manifestation of the urban utilitarianism that had defined Factory's early visual programme. However, this was not a theme-club based on the label's industrial chic – rather, it was a sophisticated set of codes that allowed patrons to engage in design as never before. All the obvious devices used to attract people to a club were ignored – so, instead of the usual neon signage, the name of the club was carved into a small granite plaque embedded into the brick exterior wall. Entry to the club was through two black doors with the numbers '5' and '1' punched through. Inside, a theatrical lighting system was installed to allow the ambiance of the club to be varied. Despite the extensive renovations undertaken, however, Factory only had leasehold on the building, which was an extremely risky proposition. The club routinely lost money in the early years, and did not reach its peak until the acid house explosion of the late 1980s, when it firmly established itself as the flagship of club culture. Peter Saville probably came closest when he stated that 'instead of being a monument to the 80s, [The Haçienda] is the birthplace of the 90s.'

Fac 51 The Haçienda in 1985 / Des: Ben Kelly Design

Fac 51 The Haçienda / Des: Ben Kelly Design

The Gay Traitor was the cocktail bar located in the basement of The Haçienda. Its provocative name referred to Anthony Blunt, the British art historian who had spied for the Soviet Union. Two other bars on the first floor were named after Blunt's fellow spies, Kim Philby and Hicks (the cover name for Guy Burgess). The Haçienda became a meeting point for musicians and creative people involved in the Manchester scene, as well as those directly involved with Factory. The cover art for Fact 65, A Certain Ratio's *I'd Like to See You Again*, features an image of the band taken from the stairwell looking down into the bar.

Fact 65 A Certain Ratio *I'd Like to See You Again* / LP / 1982 /
Des: Kennedy's Studio, AGIDI / Ph: Andrew Haslam

Fac 51 The Haçienda, The Gay Traitor / Bar / 1982 / Des: Ben Kelly Design

Fac 51 The Haçienda, The Gay Traitor / Poster / 1982 / Des: Uncredited
Fac 51 The Haçienda / Membership Application and Card / 1982 / Des: Peter Saville & Brett Wickens

THE GAY TRAITOR

for Cocktails

VODKA: BLACK RUSSIAN; Vodka, Tia Maria, Coke. HARVEY WALLBANGER; Vodka, Orange Juice, Galliano. BLUE LAGOON; Vodka, Blue Curacao, Lemonade. **GIN:** SINGAPORE SLING; Gin, Cherry Brandy, Lemon & Sugar. SLOE COMFORTABLE SCREW; Sloe Gin, Southern Comfort, Orange. **WHISKY:** SCARLET O'HARA; Southern Comfort, Apricot Brandy, Lime. MANHATTAN; Rye, Sweet/Dry Martini & Bitters. TOM COLLINS; 2 Whisky, and B/lemon. **TEQUILA:** MARGUERITA; Tequila, Cointreau, Lemon, Salted Rim. TEQUILA SUNRISE; Tequila, Orange Juice, Grenadine. MEXICAN RED; Tequila, Vodka, Red Wine. **BRANDY:** BOSOM CARESSER; Brandy, Grand Marnier, Grenadine. KNOCKOUT DROP; Brandy, Drambuie, Lemonade. **RUM:** JAMAICA INN; Bacardi, Creme-de-Banane, Orange Juice. RUM PUNCH; Rum, Brandy, Lemon and Soda. **PASTIS:** CLOCKWORK ORANGE; Ricard, Cointreau, Orange Juice, Grenadine. **LIQUEUR:** GOLDEN CADILLAC; Cointreau, Creme-de-Cacao, Galliano, Orange Juice. OLD FASHIONED; Benedictine, Cointreau, Lemon Juice, Bitters. SOUTHERN DAZE; Southern Comfort, Cointreau, Orange Juice. SNOWBALL; Advocaat, Lime, Lemonade. **FRESH CREAM:** ALEXANDRE; Cream, Brandy, Creme-de-Cacao. GRASSHOPPER; Cream, Brandy, Creme-de-Menthe. SATIN SLIPPER; Cream, Blue Curacao, Vodka, Cointreau. PINA COLADA; Cream, Bacardi, Pineapple, Coco-Ribe. AMERICAN PIE; Cream, Cherry Brandy, Vodka. **WINE:** Red and White Wine, Lime and Lemonade. BUCKS FIZZLE; Orange Juice & Sparkling Wine. **KILLER COCKTAILS:** KILLER ZOMBIE; Rum, Vodka, Apricot Brandy, Lemon, Pineapple. ZERO HOUR; Brandy, Apricot Brandy, Creme-de-Menthe, Pernod. DEATH IN THE AFTERNOON; Pernod, Jim Beam, Sparkling Wine. MOLOTOV; Petrol, Rag, Milk Bottle. JUMPING JACK FLASH; Amphetamine & Barbiturates.

THE
KIM PHILBY BAR — H I C K S
AT FAR END OF MAIN SPACE FOR — LEFT SIDE OF BALCONY FOR
DRAUGHT BEER SHORTS, AND SOFT DRINKS — CANNED BEER FROM BIZARRE LOCATIONS

The Haçienda generated a considerable amount of printed ephemera, and the development of The Haçienda's visual identity by Peter Saville and Brett Wickens became as important as the physical construction of the club. The logotype incorporated a cedilla so as to subliminally subvert the letter 'c' into a numeral '5' – with the following letter 'I', it would then read as '51', another reference to the club's Factory catalogue number. Over the next fifteen years the club's signifiers (especially the yellow and black hazard stripes) would be adapted to a plethora of promotional material, such as this poster for the Temperance Club night.

TEMPERANCE CLUB

EVERY THURSDAY · THE HAÇIENDA
9PM-2AM · ADMISSION £1

25% OFF PRICE OF DRINKS
FREE BUS HOME TO CAMPUS / HALLS OF RESIDENCE

ORANGE JUICE · JAMES · THE WOODENTOPS · B52s · THE SMITHS · CABARET VOLTAIRE · CHAKK · ACR · TROUBLE FUNK · RUN DMC · JACKSON 5 · THE PASTELS · THE FALL · ELVIS PRESLEY · NEW ORDER · TACK HEAD · BEATLES · DJ HEDD

11/13 WHITWORTH STREET WEST MANCHESTER TEL: 061 236 5051

Fac 51 The Haçienda *Temperance Club* / Poster / 1986 / Des: Uncredited

A Certain Ratio

Knife Slits Water

FAC 57
Minny Pops

Secret story
Island

Fac 62 A Certain Ratio *Knife Slits Water* / 7-inch / 1982 / Des: Uncredited

Fac 57 Minny Pops *Secret Story* / 7-inch / 1982 / Des: RvM

Mark Farrow's design for Stockholm Monsters' second single continued to push the boundaries of 7-inch packaging. The band supplied the image of actor Montgomery Clift, which Farrow then set about colouring in a style similar to Andy Warhol's screen prints of movie stars. The sleeve opens vertically like an envelope to reveal the disk within, while the label copy was set as a paragraph of text to be read as opposed to the obligatory notes often ignored. While the sleeve is unquestionably unique, however, it came at a financial cost to the band, not least because Farrow specified five spot colours for the printing.

This is a Factory Record featuring two songs by the Stockholm Monsters.
The first of these is "Happy Ever After" which is followed by "Soft Babies" on Side B. They were recorded at Strawberry Studios and Produced by Bo-Music. Both songs were written by the Stockholm Monsters & published by East 61st Street. The sleeve was designed by Mark Farrow & printed by James Upton. The catalogue number is Fac 58.

Fac 58 Stockholm Monsters *Happy Ever After* / 7-inch / 1982 / Des: Mark Farrow

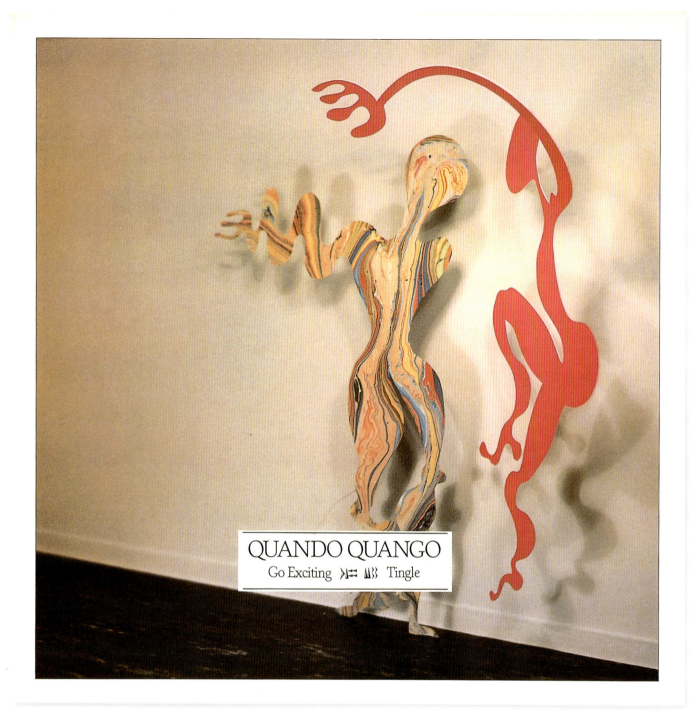

Fac **67** Quando Quango *Go Exciting/Tingle* / 12-inch / 1982 / Des: Alan David-Tu

Fact **60** The Wake *Harmony* / LP / 1982 / Des: James Kay & The Wake
Fact **70** Swamp Children *So Hot* / LP / 1982 / Des: Ann Quigley
Fbn **21** Swamp Children *So Hot* / LP / 1982 / Des: Ann Quigley

Ikon was established by Factory in 1981 in partnership with filmmaker Malcolm Whitehead, and until 1987 was run from the Factory offices at Palatine Road and a specially designed bunker in Tony Wilson's cellar. Brian Nicholson joined Ikon in 1982 with the opening of The Haçienda. Ikon specialized in video releases that were included in the Factory catalogue and in their own inventory. Content predominantly consisted of music videos and live footage of bands. These two releases feature flip-top packaging, similar to cigarettes; most of the design was handled by Whitehead and Wilson, who adapted the preexisting Factory iconography and visual codes.

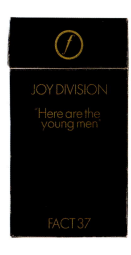

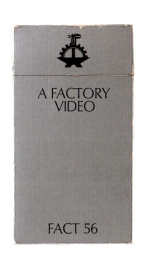

Fact 37 Joy Division *Here are the Young Men* / Video / 1982 / Des: Malcolm Whitehead & Tony Wilson
Fact 56 Various Artists *A Factory Video* / Video / 1982 / Des: Malcolm Whitehead & Tony Wilson

Blue Monday is arguably the most famous sleeve in the Factory story, not to mention in popular culture. Saville designed this sleeve based on the 5.25-inch floppy discs which were used in electronic music production. The designer grasped the significance of this form in parallel with the technologically advanced nature of the track itself, which would go on to become the best-selling 12-inch of all time. All the track information, including title and catalogue number, is communicated via the colour bars on the right-hand side. This can be deciphered using the colour wheel on the reverse of Fact 75 (see p. 65). Due to the use of die-cutting and specified colours, the production cost of this sleeve was so high that the single sold at a loss. Later reissues had subtle changes to limit the cost.

Fac 73 New Order *Blue Monday* / 12-inch / 1983 / Des: Peter Saville & Brett Wickens

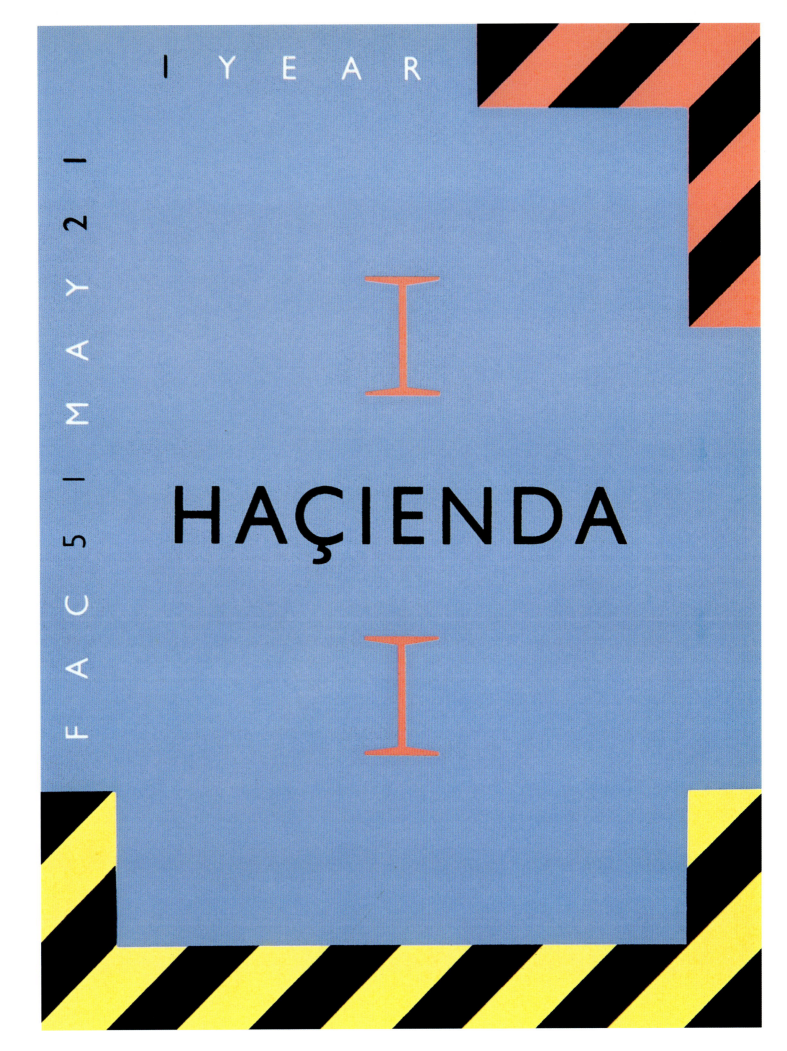

Fac 83 *Haçienda 1 Year* / Poster / 1983 / Des: Peter Saville Associates (PSA)

The sleeve of *Power, Corruption & Lies* is an ironic juxtaposition of old and new worlds, in which a reproduction of Henri Fantin-Latour's *A Basket of Roses* (1890) is combined with a colour control bar indicative of 20th-century reprographics. Saville had originally set out to find an image of a Machiavellian tyrant, but found this image more suggestive. Saville had seen contemporary Dutch designer Gert Dumbar include printing marks as a graphic device, but he took the conceit further by using the colour bar as a graphic code to replace any obvious lettering on the sleeve. Each colour is a letter or number, which can be translated using the decoding device on the back cover. The idea to lift Fantin-Latour's painting came from contemporary designers who were fashioning clothes from chintz upholstery.

DURUTTI *I Get Along Without You Very Well* COLUMN

These two sleeves demonstrate the different approaches taken by Mark Farrow in his early work for Factory. The sleeve for Fac 64 was designed to evoke a cinematic experience, with the central image taken from a short film featuring Lindsay Reade, Tony Wilson's then wife. This image runs in a panoramic strip across the sleeve with the title set to resemble subtitles at the bottom of a film screen. Fac 68, meanwhile, is a compositional exercise in the use of letterforms, shapes and metallic inks.

Section 25 · Back To Wonder · Beating Heart · Fac 68

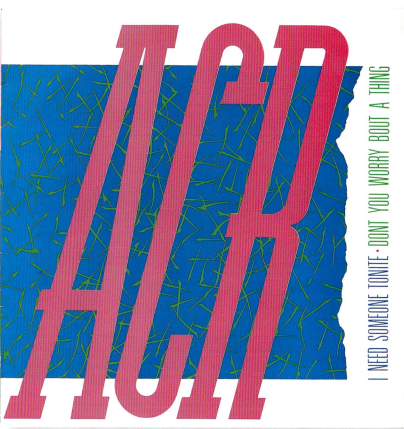

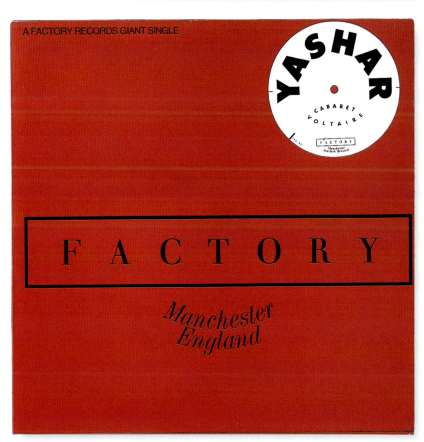

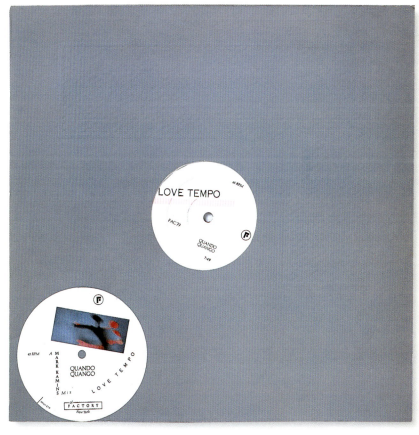

Fbn 23 Quando Quango *Love Tempo* / 12-inch / 1983 / Des: Alan David-Tu
Fac 82 Cabaret Voltaire *Yashar* / 12-inch / 1983 / Label Des: Mark Holt / Sleeve Des: Tony Wilson

Fac 72 A Certain Ratio *I Need Someone Tonite* / 12-inch / 1983 / Des: Mark Farrow
Fac 79 Quando Quango *Love Tempo* / 12-inch / 1983 / Des: Uncredited / Ph: Alan David-Tu

Confusion again employs the colour-bar device of Fac 73 (see p. 62) and
Fact 75 (see p. 64), though this time the lettering itself is made up of colour
pixels, in a state of disorder. The enlarged '93' is the most recognizable
form on the cover, and clearly refers to the catalogue number. The flickering
digital letters, suspended in time, are based on registration strips found on
offset printing proofs used to gauge the accuracy of colours on press.

Fac 93 New Order *Confusion* / 12-inch / 1983 / Des: PSA

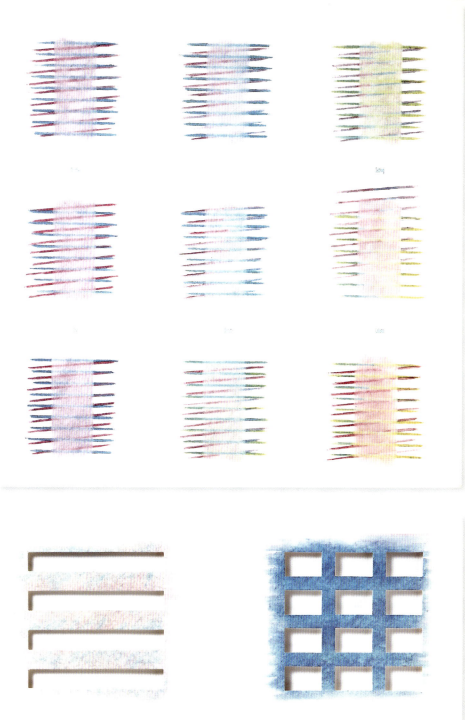

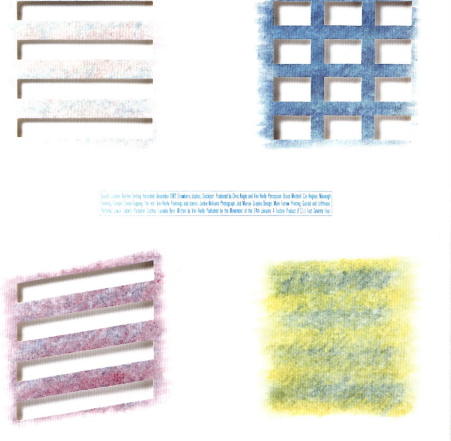

James's self-produced cover stands in stark contrast to the refined design sensibility that exudes from other Factory artwork. The naive felt-pen lettering may seem brutish compared to the work of Saville, but it does successfully complement the folk essence of the music while demonstrating the band's desire to deviate from the Factory aesthetic – and the label's acceptance of this. The band members originally agreed to choose a sleeve after each of them had come up with a drawing. However, only the bassist, Jim Glennie, completed the task.

Fac 78 James *Jimone* / 7-inch / 1983 / Des: James

For their second single, The Wake chose to appropriate El Lissitzky's *Beat the Whites with the Red Wedge* lithograph designed in 1919. Although there is no thematic link with the recording, it is an example of a common stylistic borrowing of Soviet Constructivist graphics during the early 1980s.

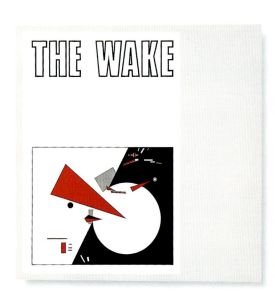

Fbn 24 The Wake *Something Outside* / 12-inch / 1983 / Des: Jackie Gribbon & The Wake

Fact 71 Various Artists *A Factory Outing* / Video / 1983 / Des: Malcolm Whitehead
Fact 77 New Order *Taras Shevchenko* / Video / 1983 / Des: PSA
Fact 89 John Dowie *Dowie* / Video / 1983 / Des: Malcolm Whitehead / Illustration: Ralph Steadman

Fac 81 *Factory First International Congress* / Notepaper / 1983 / Des: Tony Wilson

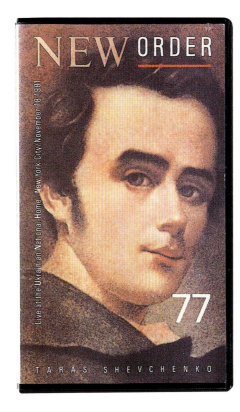

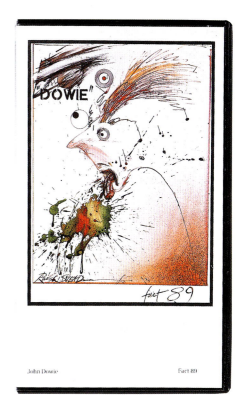

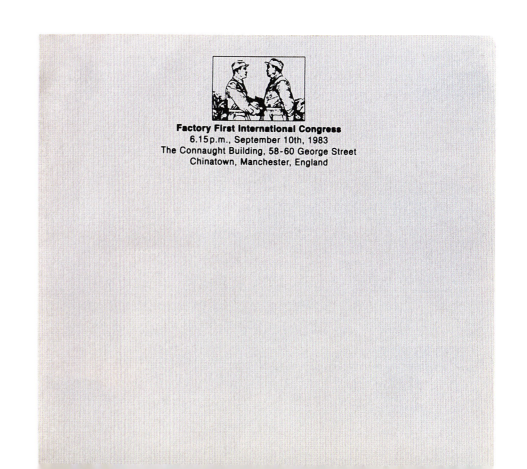

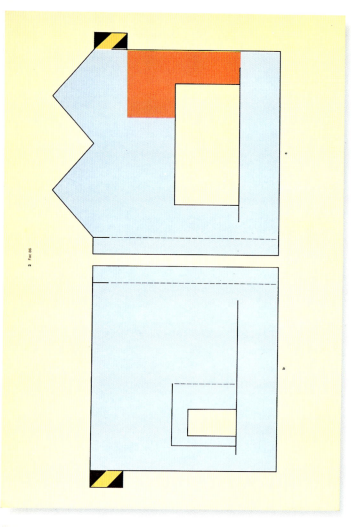

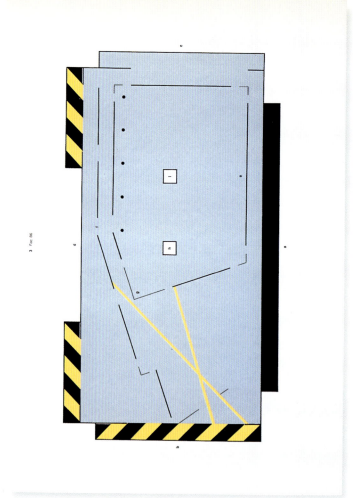

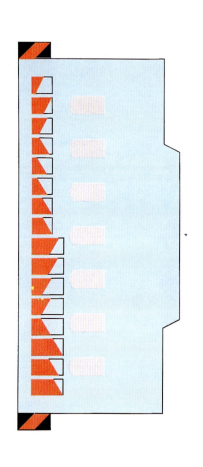

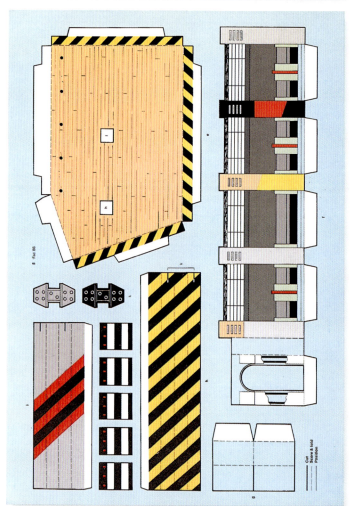

Each year Factory commissioned special Christmas gifts to be sent to associates, business partners and other key industry figures, and this tradition was maintained throughout the label's lifetime. In the mid-80s, Tony Wilson commissioned Johnson Panas to create a cardboard model kit of The Haçienda nightclub. Sections were cut out of four sheets of card, bound with a covering card and autographed cigar band. Later gifts took different forms, including Fac 145, a CD card case, in 1985 (see p. 97), Fac 245, a set of 'Madchester' postcards, in 1989 (see p. 174), and Fac 295, a photo print of Factory HQ, in 1990 (see p. 190).

Fac 88 The Wake *Talk About the Past* / 12-inch / 1984 / Des: Jackie Gribbon & The Wake

The Wake was one of the few bands that took responsibility for their own artwork, though in this case the band clearly allowed the label catalogue number to take precedence over their name and title. The Wake were conscious of Factory's visual identity and decided to align themselves with the brand – this stands in stark contrast with several of the bands who, given the opportunity, tried to resist the Factory mark.

Fac 97 Streetlife *Act on Instinct* / 12-inch / 1984 / Des: Tom Mulder & Ron van Roon
Fac 102 Quando Quango *Atom Rock* / 12-inch / 1984 / Des & Ph: Alan David-Tu

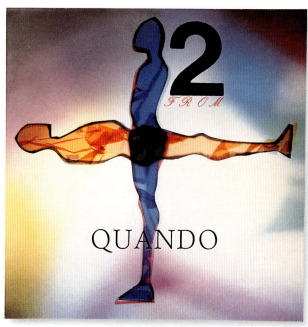

This sleeve continues the visual coding of Facs 73 and 93 and Fact 75, though in this case the colour codes are shot in camera as an installation. Photographed in the hills of Snowdonia, in Wales, by Trevor Key and Peter Saville, each stick is coloured to represent the catalogue number, name and artist – a logical progression from the flat, two-dimensional strategies of the preceding releases. This album was produced by Bernard Sumner of New Order and the designer represented his involvement through the continuation of these visual codes. The poles, suggestive of surveying, are a reference to the name of the band in terms of a division of the land's surface.

Previous spread: Fac 120 Factory Logo / 1984 / Des: PSA
Facus 21 Factory Logo / 1984 / Des: Chris Mathan

Christmas 1984 / Poster & Sticker / 1984 / Des: PSA

Fac 126 *Alan Goes to Moscow* / Poster / 1984 / Des: PSA

This poster was designed to represent the notion of Factory's expanding production range and distribution network. Using Isotypes, each symbol is a pictorial representation of the label's activities. The top row represents Factory and its records; beneath are a windmill, signifying Brussels (the base of the label's offshoot Factory Benelux), and a ship standing for overseas. The last row features a camera to represent Ikon (Factory's video wing – see p. 61), and a computer disc for software and new technologies. The first symbol became the new Factory logo in 1984, maintaining the industrial aesthetic. It was adopted by the label's US offshoot later that year, though the smoke bellowing from the chimney was replaced by a star and stripes. If the original version is rotated 90 degrees it bears a resemblance to a cigar-smoking factory owner. The pictographs were also used on a poster and sticker for Christmas 1984.

Thieves Like Us continues Saville's journey through 20th-century visual culture, though it also marks the end of his deliberate referencing of non-contemporary material. Described by the designer as an attempt to 'create a metaphysical photograph', the primary reference is Italian Surrealist painter Giorgio De Chirico's *Le Mauvais Génie d'un roi* (The king's evil genius, c. 1914–15). Photographed by Trevor Key, the concept was carried across to the follow-up release *Murder* on the Factory Benelux offshoot. The numbers on the front of Fac 103 are derived from an antique table found in Blair Castle, Scotland, which Saville had seen in a magazine. It is worth noting that the number 7 is missing – perhaps not a coincidence that it was the seventh release for the band.

Fac 103 New Order *Thieves Like Us* / 12-inch / 1984 / Des: PSA / Ph: Trevor Key
Fbn 22 New Order *Murder* / 12-inch / 1984 / Des: PSA / Ph: Trevor Key

Fac 111 Shark Vegas *You Hurt Me* / 12-inch / 1984 / Des: Mark Farrow

Fact 95 Royal Family & The Poor *The Project – Phase 1 (The Temple of the 13th Tribe)* / LP / 1984 / Des: Trevor Johnson / Artwork: Mike Keane

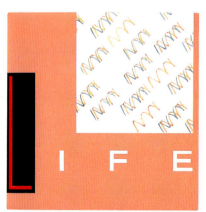

Fbn 34 Lavolta Lakota *Prayer* / 7-inch / 1984 / Des: Uncredited
Fac 96 Ad Infinitum *Telstar* / 7-inch / 1984 / Des: Mark Farrow

Fac 107 Stockholm Monsters *National Pastime* / 7-inch / 1984 / Des: Trevor Johnson
Fac 106 Life *Tell Me* / 7-inch / 1984 / Des: Mark Farrow

Without Mercy was the first project for Mark Holt and Simon Johnston under the name 8vo. They were approached after Saville had made little progress with the sleeve and the label needed to get the job done. The image by Henri Matisse was tipped on to pulp board, with letterpressed typography added in a way reminiscent of Guillaume Apollinaire's flowing poetry. For 8vo this was an honest response to the supplied image. A similar approach would be adopted for the Durutti Column's next single (see p. 86), though there the image – a detail of a page from James Joyce's *Finnegans Wake* – was chosen by the designers. These sleeves can be considered as stepping-stones in the evolution of 8vo.

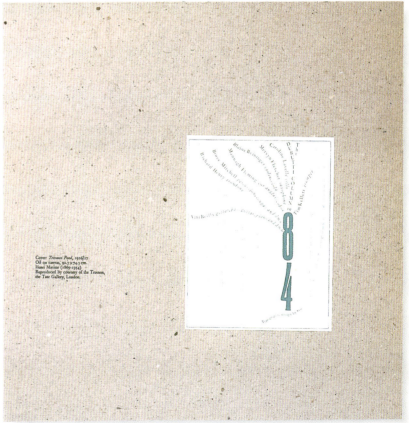

Fact 84 The Durutti Column *Without Mercy* / LP / 1984 / Des: 8vo

Fact 80 The Stockholm Monsters *Alma Mater* / LP / 1984 / Des: Trevor Johnson

Alma Mater was the first Factory release to feature the graphic work of
Trevor Johnson. The sleeve features an image of an opium smoker, chosen
by band members, and printed in a colour representing the poppy from
which the drug is derived. There are three layers of typographic content
consisting of the band's name, album title and catalogue number. The
title and number run across both the front and back cover in different
orientations. However, Johnson designed the sleeve so that it could work
both independently, and also tile together to form one large-scale display,
as above.

Too Crazy Cowboys, originally released by Factory US (Factus 16), was designed by American artist Lawrence Weiner. Weiner was commissioned by Michael Shamberg, who ran the label's transatlantic operation from New York City. Shamberg also commissioned work from a range of contemporary artists and filmmakers including John Baldessari, Robert Breer (see p. 149), Jonathan Demme, Robert Frank, Barbara Kruger, Robert Longo and William Wegman. The cover features a wedge die-cut in the top corner and is emblematic of Weiner's stark angular text and graphic work.

Fact 85 Thick Pigeon *Too Crazy Cowboys* / LP / 1984 / Des: Lawrence Weiner / Drawing: Jill

ACR wanted to make this single, *Life's a Scream*, resemble imported records from Japan, which were characterized by the use of an obi band or vertical sash with translations of the text for the Japanese market. The image, a photo of a Turkish Air Force parade, was supplied by the band. For Farrow this marked a step up to higher-profile bands on the label. A two-colour sleeve is printed with a spot varnish with a very subtle band logotype reversed under the obi band. A detail is taken from the image on the front cover and blown up on the back.

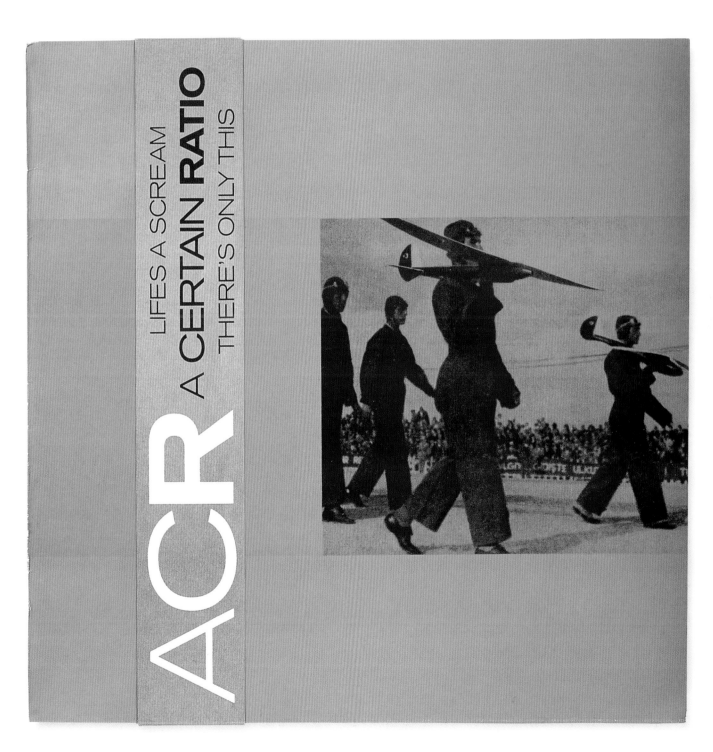

LIFES A SCREAM
A CERTAIN RATIO
THERE'S ONLY THIS

ACR

Fac 112 A Certain Ratio *Life's a Scream* / 12-inch / 1984 / Des: Mark Farrow

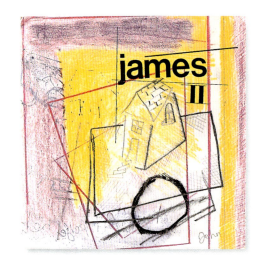
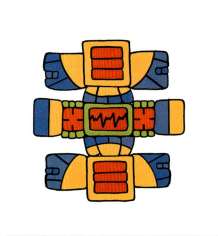

Fac 119 James *James* / 7-inch / 1985 / Des: John Carroll
Fac 122 Life *Optimism* / 7-inch / 1985 / Des: Mark Farrow
Fac 113 The Wake *Of the Matter* / 7-inch / 1985 / Des: Jackie Gribbon & The Wake

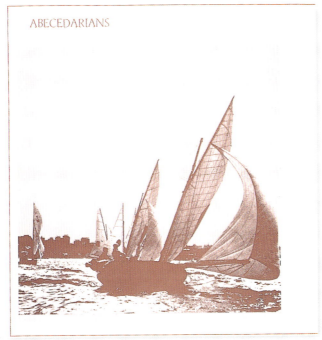

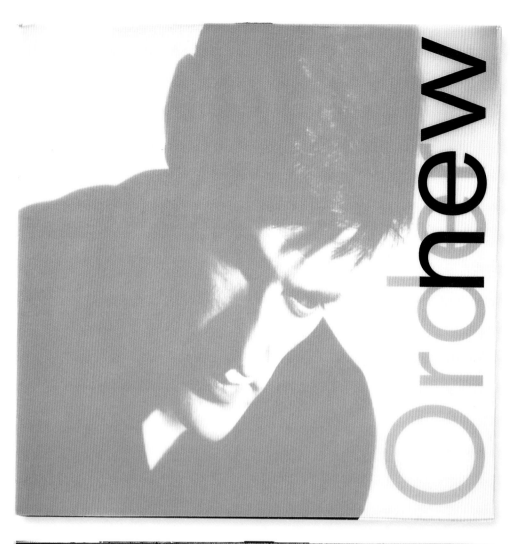

Love
vigilantes
The
perfect
kiss
This
time
of
night
Sunrise
Elegia
Sooner
than
you
think
Sub
-culture
Face
up

Low-life is the only New Order sleeve to feature portraits of the band. It is fundamentally concerned with the people making the music, a major departure from the preceding conceptually driven sleeves which had shrouded the band in every manner of code and diversionary tactic. Yet the tracing-paper sleeve adds another level of sophistication and style, and this multi-layered composition is further enhanced by the over-printed text on the cover (which is a direct quotation of Josef-Muller Brockmann's *Der Film* poster of 1960). The vertical orientation of the text was carried across to Fac 123 (see p. 91), where it is blind embossed.

Fact 100 New Order *Low-life* / LP / 1985 / Des: PSA / Ph: Trevor Key

Fact 100c	Low-life
Fact 100c	
1	
Love vigilantes	
The perfect kiss	
This time of night	
Sunrise	
The perfect kiss	New Order
(fac 123)	
2	
Elegia	
Sooner than you think	
Sub-culture	A Factory Cassette
Face up	
The kiss of death	
Perfect pit	

Fact 100c	Low-life
Fact 100c	
1	
Love vigilantes	
The perfect kiss	
This time of night	
Sunrise	
The perfect kiss	New Order
(fac 123)	
2	
Elegia	
Sooner than you think	
Sub-culture	A Factory Cassette
Face up	
The kiss of death	
Perfect pit	

Fact 100c	Low-life
Fact 100c	
1	
Love vigilantes	
The perfect kiss	
This time of night	
Sunrise	
The perfect kiss	New Order
(fac 123)	
2	
Elegia	
Sooner than you think	
Sub-culture	A Factory Cassette
Face up	
The kiss of death	
Perfect pit	

Fact 100c	Low-life
Fact 100c	
1	
Love vigilantes	
The perfect kiss	
This time of night	
Sunrise	
The perfect kiss	New Order
(fac 123)	
2	
Elegia	
Sooner than you think	
Sub-culture	A Factory Cassette
Face up	
The kiss of death	
Perfect pit	

SPINE

FRONT

PAGE 1

PAGE 2

hacienda

third anniversary celebration

(**3**) may **21** 1985

three at last

Fac 51 *Hacienda Third Anniversary* / Poster / 1985 / Des: 8vo

Large format posters were commissioned each year to promote the anniversary of The Haçienda. The first was given a catalogue number, Fac 83 (see p. 63), but thereafter they went uncatalogued. This tradition continued over the next fifteen years, until the club closed in 1997, half a decade after the label itself had folded. The poster opposite was designed by 8vo and demonstrates their move towards typographic-led communication. It is interesting to compare it to their previous sleeve for The Durutti Column, Fac 114 (see p. 86). As so often the designers rendered the typographic content in camera, offering a multi-layered reading experience.

circuses and bread

This sleeve marked a new phase for 8vo's creative team with the arrival of Hamish Muir. The piece was an entirely collaborative effort, with all three designers working simultaneously on it. Although there is a stylistic drift towards Swiss-inspired typographic composition, with sans serif fonts and solid blocks of colour, it is a logical progression from the layering and structure of 8vo's previous outings for Factory. The collage for this sleeve was shot onto 8 x 10-inch transparency and supplied to the printer in Belgium. The reproduction house was required only to enlarge the supplied image, thus greatly simplifying the handover from designer to printer.

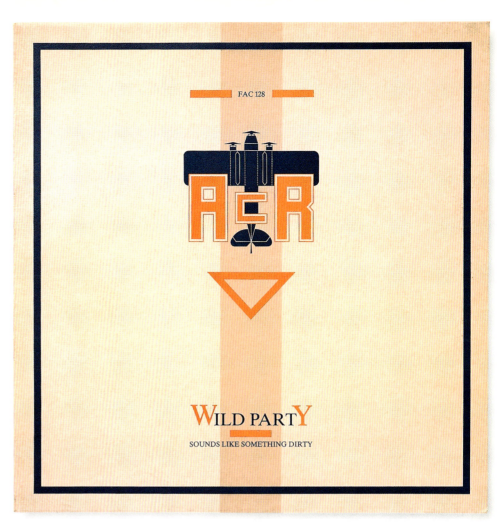

ACR wanted to continue the aviation motif of their preceding single, *Life's a Scream*, designed by Mark Farrow. In this instance, Trevor Johnson appropriated Alexander Rodchenko's cover for *Flight: Aviation Verse*, originally designed in 1923. This was inspired by a renewed interest in Soviet culture, and Russian Constructivism in particular, among contemporary designers in Britain during this period. The image on the back cover is of ACR member Jeremy Kerr's arm.

Fac 128 A Certain Ratio *Wild Party* / 12-inch / 1985 / Des: Trevor Johnson

Fbn 46 Stockholm Monsters *How Corrupt is Rough Trade?* / 12-inch / 1985 / Des: Trevor Johnson

STOCKHOLM MONSTERS

HOW CORRUPT IS ROUGH TRADE?
KAN KILL!

45 RPM

PRODUCED BY BE-MUSIC

RECORDED AT SUITE 16 ROCHDALE

WRITTEN BY STOCKHOLM MONSTERS.

PUBLISHED BY HETGERUCHT

SLEEVE – TJ

FBN 46

Trevor Johnson's original design for this single was to have featured only the punctuation marks from both song titles – '?' and '!' respectively. The character forms were enlarged to exceed the boundary of the cover, and minimal tracklisting and credits were added on the reverse. The boldness of the original composition was enhanced by the addition, at the request of the band, of a found period photograph, which was placed within the dot of the question mark. The image of a young, naked woman, in a somewhat vulnerable position, gives the sleeve a much more suggestive dimension.

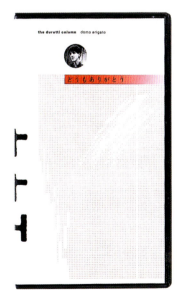

Fact 144 The Durutti Column *Domo Arigato* / Video & CD / 1985 / Des: 8vo /
Ph: Kevin Cummins, Yoshimasa Hatano, Tony Wilson

Central Station Design made an anti-design statement from the outset. They wanted to create a completely fresh look that was very much their own, in stark opposition to what they considered the over-designed output of their contemporaries. This simple sleeve featuring green hills, blue sky and birds on the horizon initially appears naive and childlike but it is very much considered. The label gave the go-ahead even though they did not fully understand it – fortunately this would be the start of a long and productive relationship.

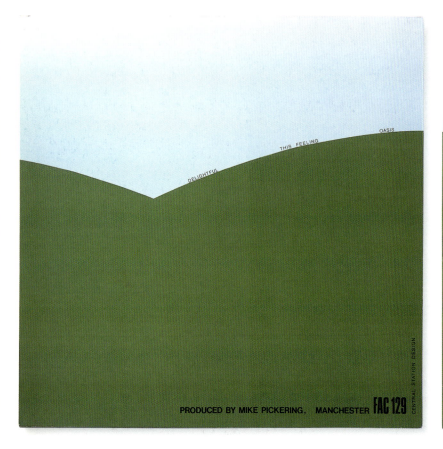

Fac 129 Happy Mondays *Delightful* / 12-inch / 1985 / Des: Central Station Design

Alan David-Tu designed several sleeves for Quando Quango, experimenting with constructed photography, which involved the creation of new realities in camera. Using the studio, props, models and lighting techniques, alternative visions became tangible. Hillegonda Rietveld, a member of Quando Quango, suggested that the cover feature a sexualized image of a male. David-Tu continued his techniques of constructed photography that he had begun with Fac 67 (see p. 60), creating an image that is evocative of the philosopher or mathematician of the ancient world, a reference to the song 'Genius' on the album.

Fact 110 Quando Quango *Pigs & Battleships* / LP / 1985 / Des & Ph: Alan David-Tu
Fac 145 *Christmas Present* / Cardboard CD & sleeve / 1985 / Des: PSA

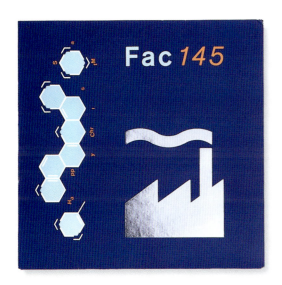

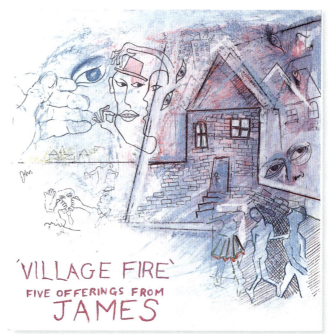

Fac 127 Kalima *Four Songs* / 12-inch / 1985 / Des: Trevor Johnson /
Painting: Clifford Saffer
Fac 138 James *Village Fire. Five Offerings From ...* / 12-inch / 1986 / Des: John Carroll

Fac 130 The Wake *Here Comes Everybody* / LP / 1985 /
Des: Jackie Gribbon & The Wake
Fac 134 Biting Tongues *Trouble Hand* / 12-inch / 1986 / Des: Johnson Panas

Fact 135 A Certain Ratio *The Old & The New* / LP & 7-inch / 1986 / Des: Johnson Panas

Fac 147 Kalima *Whispered Words* / 12-inch / 1986 / Des: Trevor Johnson /
Woodcut: Clifford Saffer
Fact 155 Kalima *Night Time Shadows* / LP / 1986 / Des: Trevor Johnson /
Woodcut: Clifford Saffer

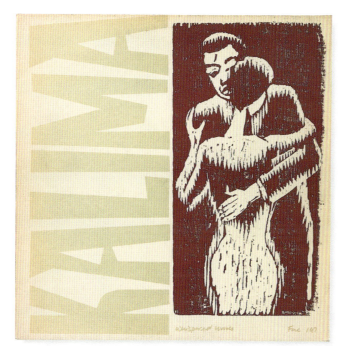

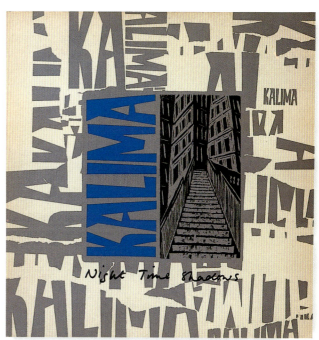

The key image of *Shellshock* is actually the wall of a workshed used by tradesmen to clean their paintbrushes. The photograph, taken by Geoff Power, was akin to 'real-life' abstract expressionism. Saville saw this non-aware aesthetic as entirely suitable for the sleeve. The leaden tones were also suggestive of a battlefield environment relating to the song's title. Rectangular in orientation, the image was cropped for the cover but continues across the insert. The only primary typographic content is the name of the single and Factory catalogue number – the name New Order does not appear on the sleeve itself. This was yet another example of the diversionary tactics employed by Saville that gave the band the reputation for being mysterious and guarded.

Fac 143 New Order *Shellshock* / 12-inch / 1986 / Des: PSA / Ph: Geoff Power

Fac 143 New Order *Shellshock* / 12-inch / 1986 / Des: PSA / Ph: Geoff Power

shellshock

A Factory Communications product.

143

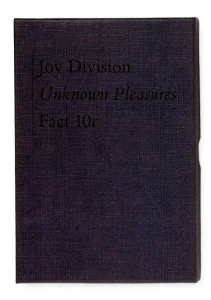

Joy Division
Unknown Pleasures
Fact 10c

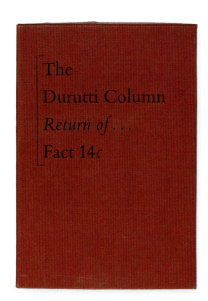

The
Durutti Column
Return of . . .
Fact 14c

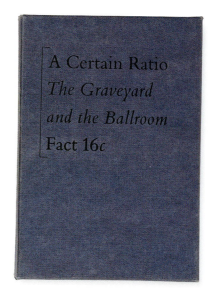

A Certain Ratio
*The Graveyard
and the Ballroom*
Fact 16c

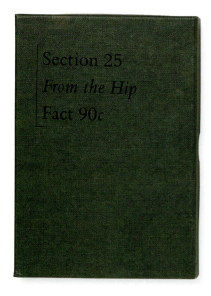

Quando Quango
Pigs and Battleships
Fact 110c

Happy Mondays
*Squirrel & G-Man
Twenty-Four Hour
Party People
Plastic Face Carn't
Smile (White Out)*
Fact 170c

Wim Mertens
Educes Me
Fact 190c

Section 25
From the Hip
Fact 90c

Fact 90c   1
© 1986 Factory Communications Limited

From 1984 Factory released a series of special edition cassettes in their own custom packaging designed by Peter Saville Associates. Individual board boxes housed a tape that sat within a tray accompanied by artwork. These were originally designed to work as a set, with each colour coded for the respective artist or band. A total of twenty-two cassettes were released in the series before Factory discontinued them in 1987. These objects were another example of the label's willingness to produce unique items that went beyond normal expectations.

Factory
Communications
Limited
86 Palatine Road
Manchester
M20 9JW
England
061 434 3876
/ 445 2826
Telex 669 009
Facman G

fac 141

Directors:
Alan Erasmus
Tina Simmons
Anthony Wilson
Consultant:
Peter Saville
Registered in England
No 1524272
Vat No 3832 66632

45 RPM

THE ROYAL FAMILY & THE POOR
side a : we love the moon
side b : white stains
fac 139
copyright - the project 1986

dedicated to all those involved in the struggle.
who feels it knows it. love in the law. love under will.
written & arranged by mike keane.

THE
ROYAL
FAMILY
&
THE
POOR

we love the moon

Haçienda 51

4

21 May 1986

Fourth Birthday

8vo was given another opportunity to experiment with pure typography in this poster commission. However, despite the implicit freedom that came with such an open brief, it was handled with the same rigorous methodology and thinking that the team would apply to a more formal project. The final design was the outcome of considerable testing and experimentation, with the team balancing both introspective concerns and communicative objectives. The composition took three weeks to resolve.

Fac 51 *Haçienda Fourth Birthday* / Poster / 1986 / Des: 8vo

Challenging the viewer's interpretation of colour and shape, Central Station return to the similar landscape of the preceding Fac 129 single (see p. 96), though here the colours are intensified and a writhing insect-like creature takes over the foreground. Central Station Design received a degree of criticism from contemporaries for their work, particularly their use of colour, but the label appreciated its relevance and difference, especially given the unprecedented nature of the band. These were the primary stages in the evolution of a new visual language.

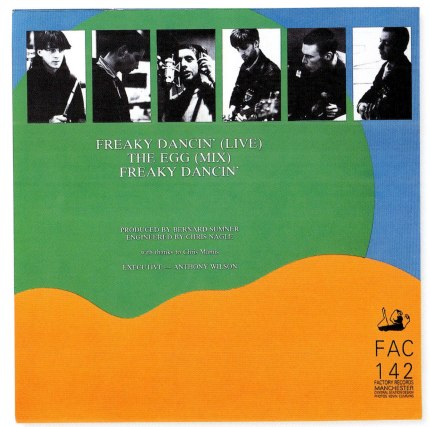 

Fac 142 Happy Mondays *Freaky Dancin'* / 12-inch / 1986 / Des: Central Station Design / Ph: Kevin Cummins

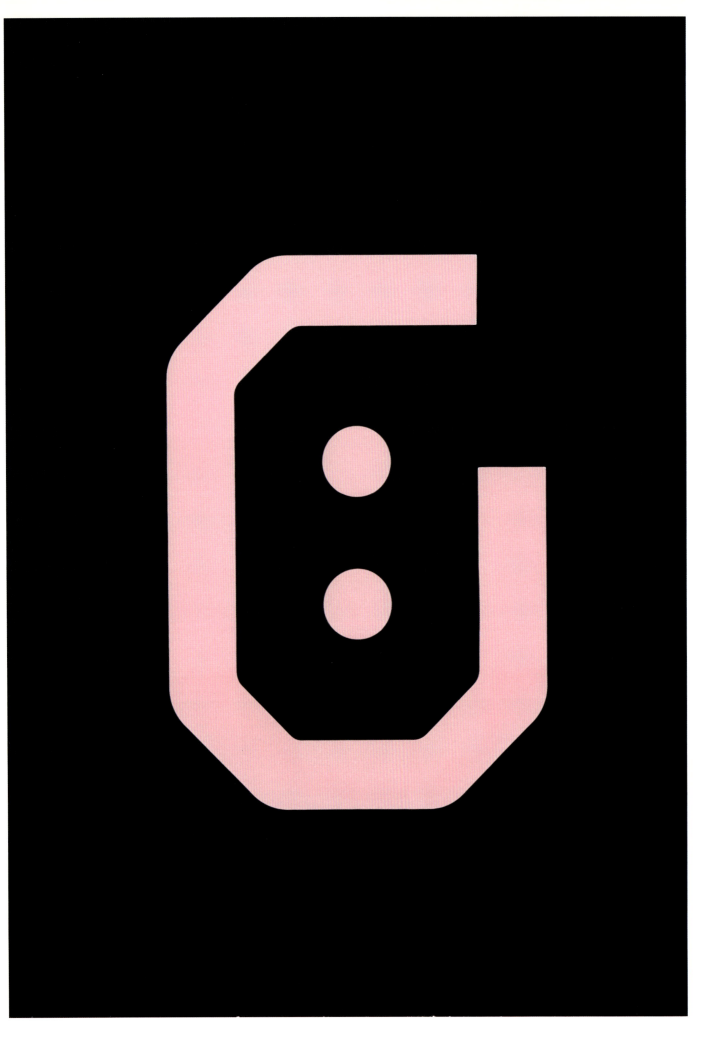

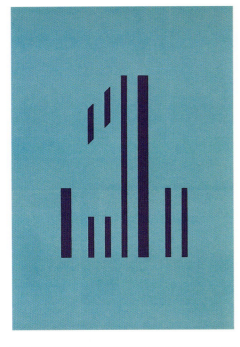

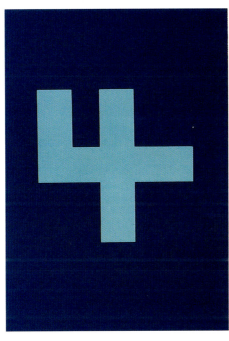

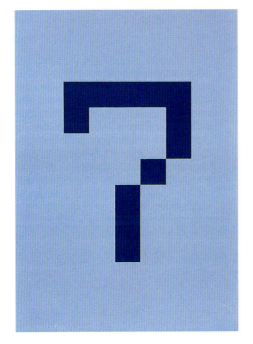

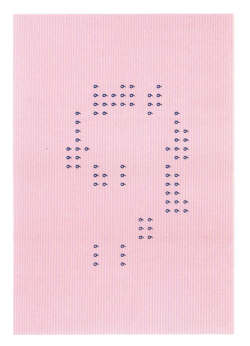

Fac 151 *Festival of the 10th Summer Number Set* / Postcards / 1986 / Des: PSA

In 1986, Factory initiated a project to celebrate the Sex Pistols' 1976 visit to Manchester which had left such an indelible mark on the city's cultural landscape. This festival featured a programme of events that included concerts and exhibitions. Peter Saville Associates developed a range of customized numerals to represent each year in the decade that had passed. These were used in a poster campaign that counted down the weeks leading up to the festival, as well as in a range of other promotional materials. The numbers were also recreated as three-dimensional typographic sculptures exhibited at the Manchester City Gallery. An anniversary poster (see opposite page) was designed featuring a satellite image of Britain with Manchester marked with an orange cross at the bottom of the page.

Fac 151 *Festival of the 10th Summer* / Installation / 1986 / Des: PSA / Ph: Trevor Key

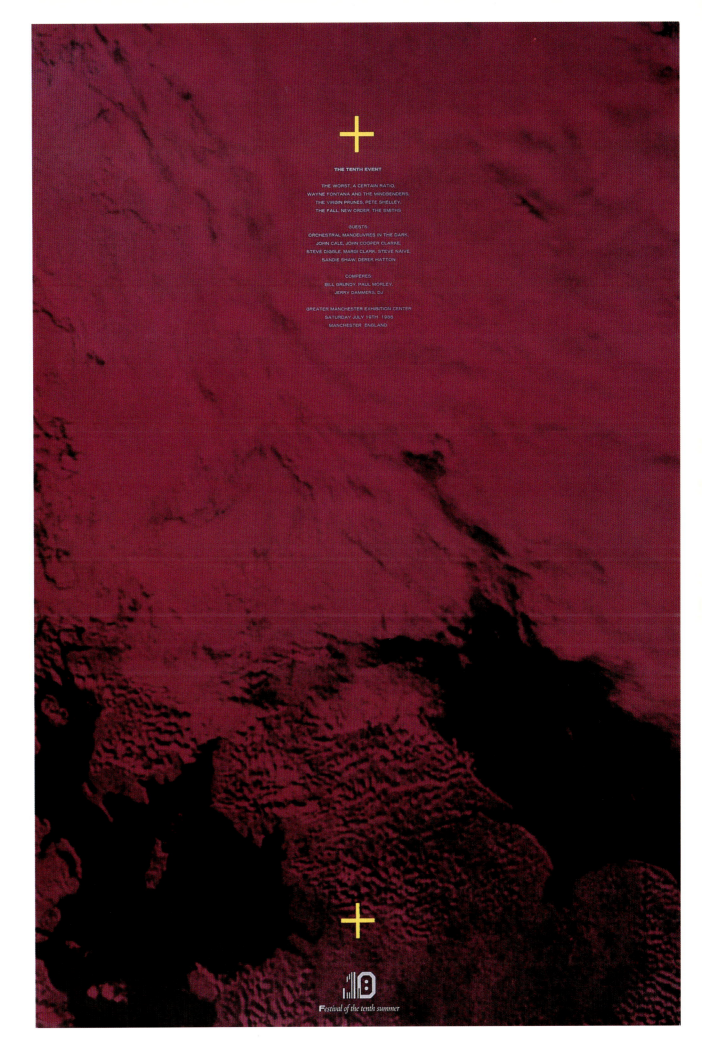

THE TENTH EVENT

THE WORST, A CERTAIN RATIO,
WAYNE FONTANA AND THE MINDBENDERS,
THE VIRGIN PRUNES, PETE SHELLEY,
THE FALL, NEW ORDER, THE SMITHS

GUESTS:
ORCHESTRAL MANOEUVRES IN THE DARK,
JOHN CALE, JOHN COOPER CLARKE,
STEVE DIGGLE, MARGI CLARK, STEVE NAIVE,
SANDIE SHAW, DEREK HATTON

COMPÈRES:
BILL GRUNDY, PAUL MORLEY,
JERRY DAMMERS, DJ

GREATER MANCHESTER EXHIBITION CENTER
SATURDAY JULY 19TH 1986
MANCHESTER ENGLAND

Festival of the tenth summer

Fact 150 New Order *Brotherhood* / LP / 1986/ Des: PSA / Ph: Trevor Key

The sleeve for *Brotherhood* typifies what Peter Saville describes as his essentialist period. This work is a conscious attempt to move away from the literal quotation of historical references – in this case by alluding to the spirit of Yves Klein's paintings of the 1950s. Klein's work explored the concept of nothingness, and was in essence reductivist. Sheets of titanium zinc, a processed material used for architectural cladding, were sourced and photographed by Trevor Key. The two New Order singles released around the same period, *State of the Nation* and *Bizarre Love Triangle* (both below), continued these explorations.

Fac 153 New Order *State of the Nation* / 12-inch / 1986 / Des: PSA / Ph: Trevor Key

Fac 163 New Order *Bizarre Love Triangle* / 12-inch / 1986 / Des: PSA / Ph: Trevor Key

BILITON TITAANZINK 0,50 / 8 059
NEN 7065 KOMO 31898 84. 1986

These were the last ACR sleeves by Johnson Panas for Factory, since the band signed to a major label in 1987. Here the designers continue the very 'Boy's Own' aesthetic that they had carried through their career, this time with cartographic, mountaineering and aviation motifs dominating the packaging. The cover for the single *Mickey Way* is an iconographic representation of a compass pointing in a north-west direction in reference to the city of Manchester located in this region of England. More recently the designer Trevor Johnson made the observation that the design and packaging had became increasingly at odds with the band's direction. This visual language would change once the act signed to A&M, and Johnson Panas were able to steer ACR in a new design direction.

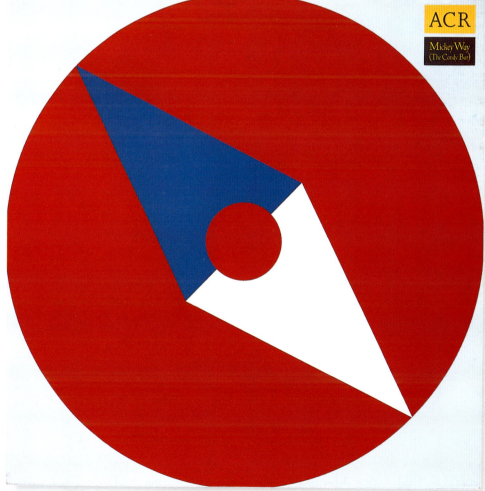

Fact 166 A Certain Ratio *Force* / LP / 1986 / Des: Johnson Panas
Fac 168 A Certain Ratio *Mickey Way (The Candy Bar)* / 12-inch /
1986 / Des: Johnson Panas
Page opposite: Fact 166 A Certain Ratio *Force* (detail of insert)

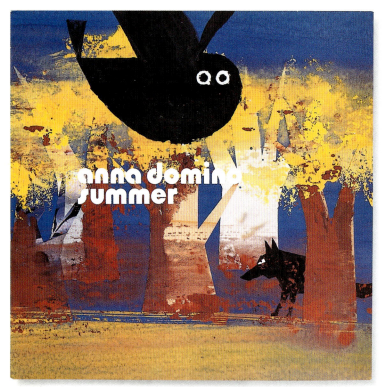

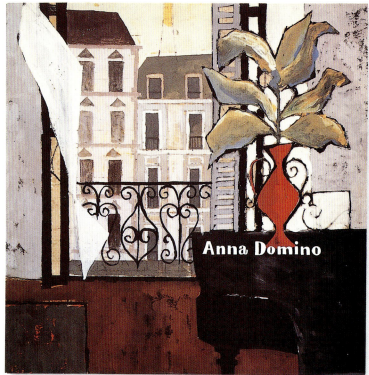

Fac 158 Anna Domino *Summer* / 12-inch / 1986 / Des: Benoit Hennebert
Fac 162 The Railway Children *A Gentle Sound* / 12-inch / 1986 / Des: Gary Newby

Fact 165 Anna Domino *Anna Domino* / LP / 1986 / Des: Benoit Hennebert
Fac 179 Miaow *When It All Comes Down* / 12-inch / 1987 / Des: Slim Smith

This sleeve hints at the densely layered collage and image-making work of Central Station's later output. The intensely acidic colour background appears to derive from a TV screen, while its horizontal emphasis evokes a sense of landscape. The overlaid painted sections were created in response to the music itself, executed with the speed and sound of the track in an attempt to capture an essence of frustration. A subtle spot varnish was run over the colour areas, leaving the black sections intentionally flat. The degraded lettering adds to the spontaneous nature of the artwork.

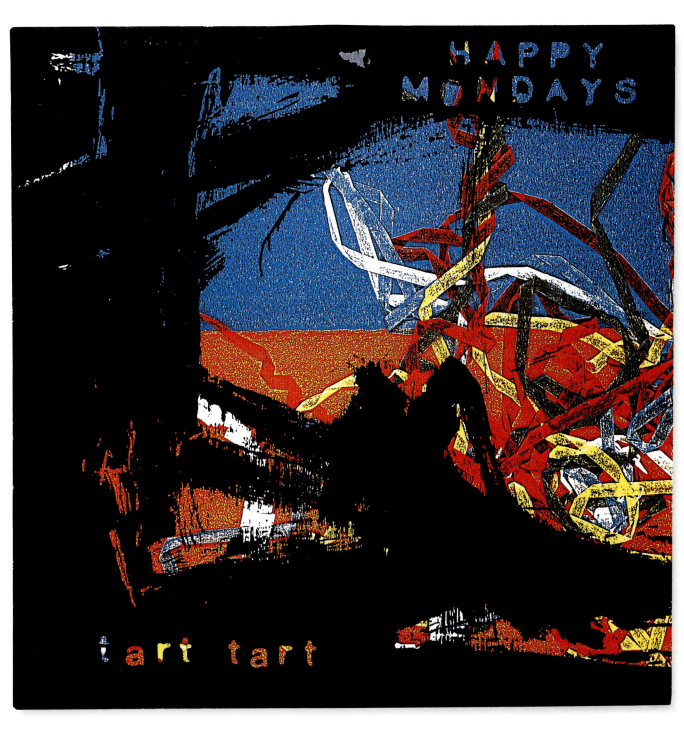

Fac **176** Happy Mondays *Tart Tart* / 12-inch / 1987 / Des: Central Station Design

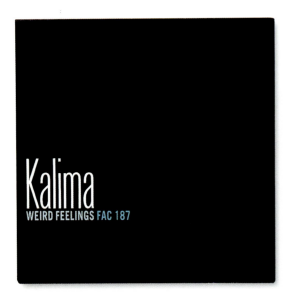

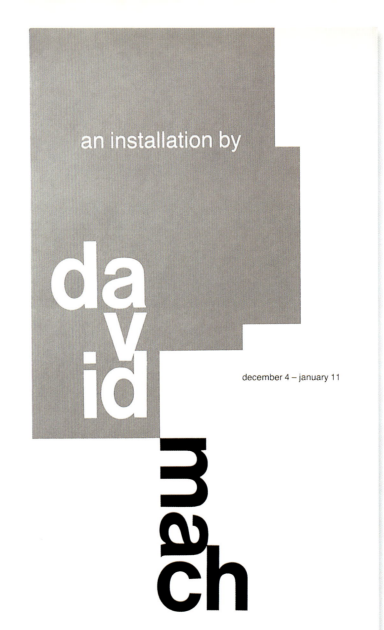

an installation by

da
v
id
mach

december 4 – january 11

fac 51

viewing by admission to club
thursday to saturday
9 am – 2 pm
admission prices as usual
for details phone 236 5051
the hacienda
11/13 whitworth street west
manchester

Fac 167 The Railway Children *Brighter* / 12-inch / 1987 / Des: Gary Newby / Ph: Mark Osborne
Fac 146 Stockholm Monsters *Party Line* / 12-inch / 1987 / Des: Johnson Panas
Fac 187 Kalima *Weird Feelings* / 12-inch / 1987 / Des: Johnson Panas

Fac 51 The Haçienda *An Installation by David Mach* / Poster / 1986 / Des: Johnson Panas

Valuable Passages was a compilation of previously released Durutti Column material, put together for the overseas market. The designers embedded the supplied image into the typographic and geometrical composition with what 8vo describe as a 'healthy disregard', making it one element within a grand 'composition'. The track listing on the back cover is a considered exercise in information 'presentation' exploiting the capabilities of the grid as a structural underpinning. This approach is continued on the inserts within.

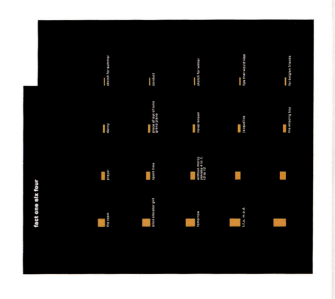

Fact 164 The Durutti Column *Valuable Passages* / Double LP / 1986 / Des: 8vo / Ph: Kevin Cummins

HAPPY MONDAYS

SQUIRREL AND G-MAN
TWENTY FOUR HOUR
PARTY PEOPLE PLASTIC FACE
CARNT SMILE (WHITE OUT)

Happy Mondays' first album sleeve features an image on the front cover, a selection of desserts, in contrast to the back cover image which is a platter of wet fish. These 'flashback' images suggest the humorous and hyperactive temperament of the band, and projects an image a thousand miles removed from the worlds of Joy Division and New Order. When Central Station Design approached the label with the idea of printing the type on a separate plastic sleeve, they expected to be knocked back considering the cost for a debut album. However, this being Factory, the label embraced the idea enthusiastically.

Fact 170 Happy Mondays *Squirrel and G-Man Twenty Four Hour Party People Plastic Face Carnt Smile (White Out)* / LP / 1987 / Des: Central Station Design

1   2   3   4   5   6   7

8   9   10   11   12   13   14

15   16   17   18   19   20   21

22   23   24   [25]   26   27   28

29   30   31   B   A   D   N

E   W   S   W   E   E   K

Bad News Week is typographically composed to represent a calendar month with pertinent information picked out. So, an entire week is marked out in reference to the title, while 25 is highlighted as the band's name. On the back the catalogue number is marked, and there is a small image of the band. Farrow is perpetuating the Factory tradition of making the audience decipher the information for themselves. The reductive treatment of the band's image is akin to Farrow's work for the Pet Shop Boys, especially the album *Please* (1986), which established his wider reputation.

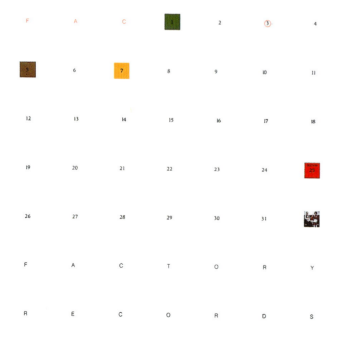

Fac 157 Section 25 *Bad News Week* / 12-inch / 1987 / Des: Mark Farrow

Fac 203 *12 Inches of New Order* / Promotional Ruler / 1987 / Des: PSA

Fac 51 *Haçienda Fifth Birthday* / Flyer / 1987 / Des: Johnson Panas

Peter Saville has said that this sleeve was one of his first ideas drawn from
real life – the precise moment of inspiration came when a leaf fell onto the
windscreen of his car at night. *True Faith* is a poetic moment frozen in time.
The image was created using the dichromat technique developed in
collaboration with Trevor Key. This process involved shooting subjects in black-
and-white film and then colouring them in camera. The blue and gold colours
again quote the work of Yves Klein (see p. 110). The motif was reworked for the
12-inch remix, as multicoloured foliage blowing across the cover.

Fac 183 New Order *True Faith* / 12-inch / 1987 / Des: PSA / Dichromat: Trevor Key & Peter Saville

Fac 183R New Order *True Faith* / 12-inch / 1987 / Des: PSA / Dichromat: Trevor Key & Peter Saville

Substance juxtaposes a rather clinical Neo-Classical type (Bodoni Titling) with vivid images of natural forms (an opening peony and a branch of coral). As with the cover for *True Faith* (see p. 122), Trevor Key and Peter Saville generated these organic images using the dichromat technique, building on Saville's desire to create 'a flower for the lobby of IBM in the year 2000'.

NEW
ORDER
—
SUBSTANCE
1987

Fact 200 New Order *Substance* / Double LP / 1987 / Des: PSA / Dichromat: Trevor Key & Peter Saville

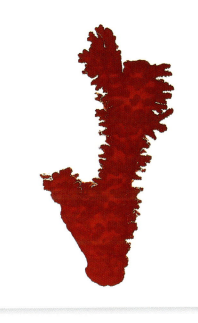

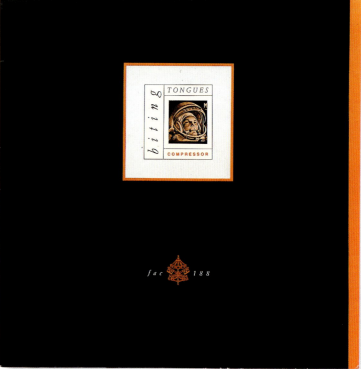

Fac 184 The Durutti Column *The City of Our Lady* / 12-inch / 1987 / Des: 8vo /
Ph: Bob Sebree

Fac 169 The Pleasure Crew *I Could Be So Good For You* / 12-inch / 1987 / Des: Realisation

Fact 190 Wim Mertens *Educes Me* / LP / 1987 / Des: Joël van Audenhaeghe / Ph: R.H.

Fac 188 Biting Tongues *Compressor* / 12-inch / 1987 / Des: Johnson Panas

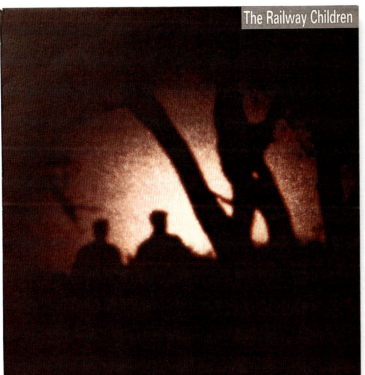

Fac 196 Meat Mouth *Meat Mouth is Murder* / 12-inch / 1987 / Des: Julie Lomax
Fact 185 The Railway Children *Reunion Wilderness* / LP / 1987 / Des: Gary Newby

Fac 178 The Wake *Something That No One Else Could Bring* / 12-inch / 1987 / Des: Realisation
Fac 192 Happy Mondays *Twenty Four Hour Party People* / 12-inch / 1987 /
Des: Central Station Design

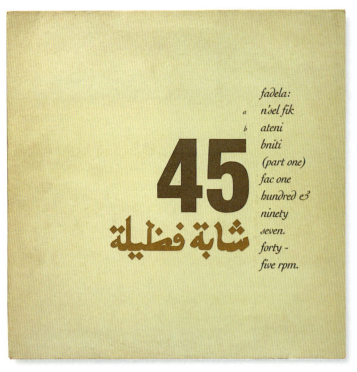

fadela:

_a n'sel fik

_b ateni
bniti
(part one)
fac one
hundred &
ninety
seven.
forty -
five rpm.

شابة فضلية

lead vocals:
chaba fadela
voice on
n'sel fik:
cheb sahraoui
all instruments
& electronics:
rachid
keyboards &
sample sounds:
samir

i could be so good for you
fac 169

pleasure crew **118 bpm**

meatmouth is murder
fac 196

meatmouth **127 bpm**

PLEASURE CREW
FAC 169
'SO GOOD'

n'sel fik
fac 197

fadela **94 bpm**

salvation
fac 182

the hood **115 bpm**

factory records
45 rpm

Fac193
Design by Peter Saville Associates.
Photography by Trevor Key
A Factory Record.

NEW
TOUCHED
BY THE
HAND
OF GOD
ORDER

In Peter Saville's opinion, the front cover for *Touched by the Hand of God* is an unresolved dichromat composition. The image continues the use of natural forms – in this instance an animal bone and conch shell. Brett Wickens's typography, meanwhile, utilizes Helvetica in contrasting weights to full effect. The layered composition is set around a sequence of connecting letterforms – these 'H's become a ladder to 'God'.

Fac 193 New Order *Touched by the Hand of God* / 12-inch / 1987 / Des: PSA / Ph: Trevor Key

FACTORY COMMUNICATIONS

In January 1978 Anthony Wilson and Alan Erasmus went into partnership trading under 'Movement of the 24th January'. Although this was focussed on the management of The Durutti Column it would lead to the foundation of Factory. To commemorate the 10th anniversary of this moment the label issued a large-format wall-planner designed by Sharon Ellis for PSA. Starting from the 24th of January the composition is methodically structured with individual days represented as single squares combining to form months in long horizontal strips. Printed in a limited edition of 200 the planner looks more like the periodic table of elements than a conventional wall chart.

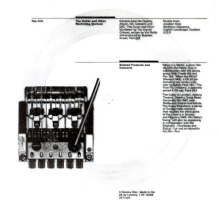

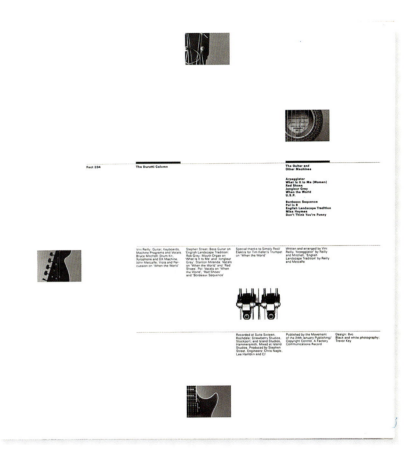

8vo developed their typical collage approach in this project by actually building a three-dimensional composition. Photographs from Trevor Key, hand-rendered typography and graphic elements were layered and photographed using a large-format camera bought by the designers especially for the project. This engaging design involved considerable testing and reworking before settling on the final version, but in the end offers a dynamic sense of depth and dimensionality that would have been difficult to produce otherwise. The back cover adopts a structured grid-based composition using more images shot by Key.

Fac 214 The Durutti Column *The Guitar and Other Marketing Devices* /
7-inch flexi-disc / 1987 / Des: 8vo / Ph: Trevor Key
Fact 204 The Durutti Column *The Guitar and Other Machines* /
LP / 1987 / Des: 8vo / Ph: Trevor Key

The Durutti Column

Fac 194 The Durutti Column *Our Lady of the Angels/When the World* / CDS / 1988 / Des: 8vo
Facd 224 The Durutti Column *The First Four Albums* / 4 x CD / 1988 / Des: 8vo

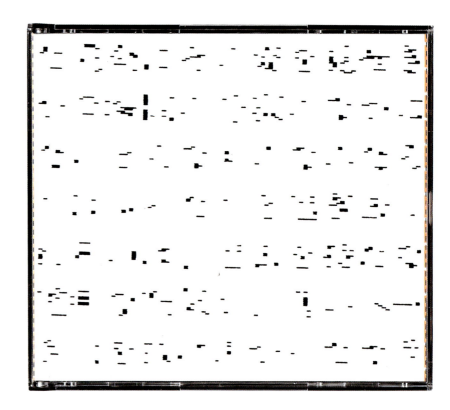

These two projects demonstrate another dimension to the work of 8vo. Instead of using the labour-intensive techniques of much of their output, these are resolved in a simple manner, with both sleeves employing randomly distorted images created by a fax machine. On the first occasion, Fac 194, the designers identified a workable section for the cover using the reproduction camera. The found image was then cropped into the shape of the sleeve. Facd 224, meanwhile, began with an image with greater inherent structure that resembled musical notation. This too was resized to work within the format. The engaging abstracted image is used on the front cover, leaving a more mannered typographic arrangement on the back cover and side of the CD case.

The Durutti Column   The First Four Albums

The Return of the Durutti Column   LC   Another Setting   Without Mercy

Facd 224

NEWORDER

Blue Monday 1988, Beach Buggy

Fac **73R** New Order *Blue Monday 1988* / 12-inch / 1988 / Des: PSA / Dichromat: Trevor Key & Peter Saville

Five years after its release Factory issued a remix of the biggest-selling 12-inch single of all time – *Blue Monday* (see p. 62). Moving away from the iconic floppy, PSA created a dichromat image that was a reasonable correspondent to the original sleeve. The artwork for *Blue Monday 1988* is a nod towards geometric abstraction, the luminous concentric circles reminiscent of the lens, or eye, of the HAL 9000 computer in Stanley Kubrick's 1968 film *2001: A Space Odyssey*.

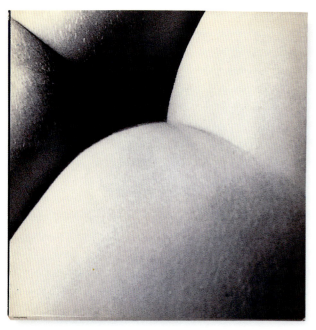

LOVE & HATE

THE BELLY
OF AN ARCHITECT
A PETER GREENAWAY FILM

Fac 198 Vermorel *Stereo/Porno* / 12-inch / 1988 / Des: PSA / Ph: Fred Vermorel

Fact 205 Jazz Defektors *Jazz Defektors* / LP / 1988 / Des: Paul Cummings / Creative Coordinator: Koichi Hanafusa / Ph: James Martin
Fact 160 Section 25 *Love & Hate* / LP / 1988 / Des: A.S.K. Design Co. / Ph: Ian Tilton

Fact 195 Wim Mertens *The Belly of an Architect* / LP / 1987 / Des: Uncredited
Fact 206 Kalima *Kalima!* / LP / 1988 / Des: Johnson Panas / Ph: James Martin

Trevor Johnson was commissioned to design the poster for the Haçienda's sixth birthday celebration. The typography for the poster was set as a justified block of text similar to a monument inscription to suggest the uncertainty of the club's future. This was adapted for the flyer, with the text photographed at an angle offering a dynamic variation on the theme. The tickets for the event (below, left) were based on materials found in the club itself. On one side the text was composed to emulate the light fixtures with black and red paint; on the reverse wood veneer is used.

Fac 51 *Haçienda Sixth Birthday* / Ticket & Flyer / 1988 / Des: Johnson Panas

JOY DIVISION
1979
⊓⊦moƨpHEſE

Peter Saville proposed the notion that Joy Division's history falls into two distinct periods: urbanism and classicism, corresponding more or less with their two albums, Fact 10, *Unknown Pleasures* (see p. 23), and Fact 25, *Closer* (see p. 29). This duality is reiterated on the sleeves of the *Substance* compilation (see pp. 138–39) and *Atmosphere* single through the use of Jan van Munster's sculptures which Saville saw as suggestive of this dynamic. It is also manifested in Brett Wickens's typographic solution that utilizes two distinctly contrasting typefaces to epitomize the old and the new worlds: Garamond, and Wim Crouwel's New Alphabet (1967).

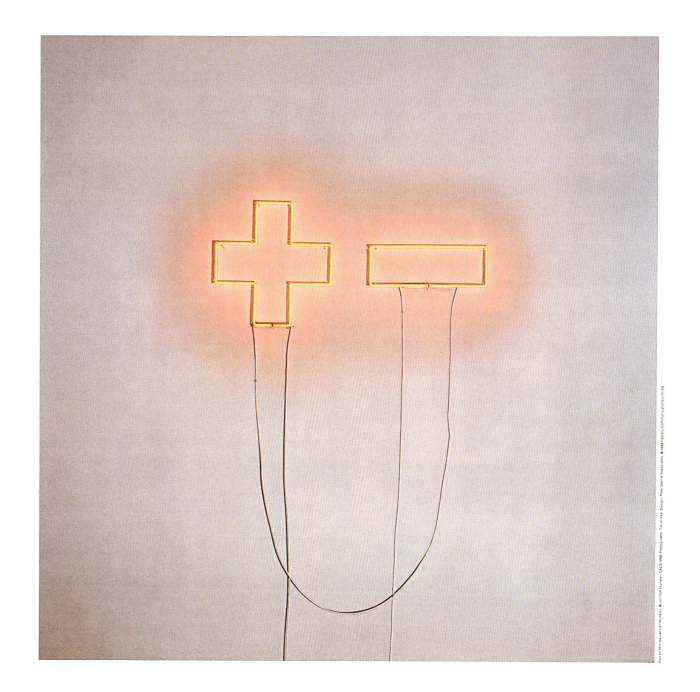

JOY DIVISION

1979

atmobphere

Fac213, Fac213/7, Facd213, Facdv213.

JOY DIVISION
1977-1980
substance

Fact250, Fact250c, Facd250, Fact250d.

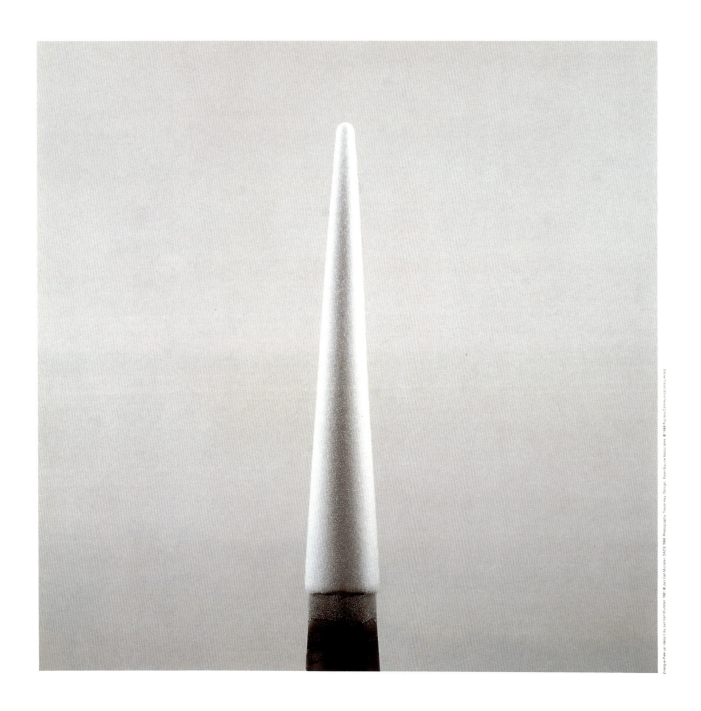

Fact 250 Joy Division *Substance* / LP & Poster / 1988 / Sculpture: *Energie-Piek Ijs* (detail) by Jan van Munster, 1981 /
Des: PSA / Art Direction: Peter Saville / Ph: Trevor Key / Typography: Brett Wickens

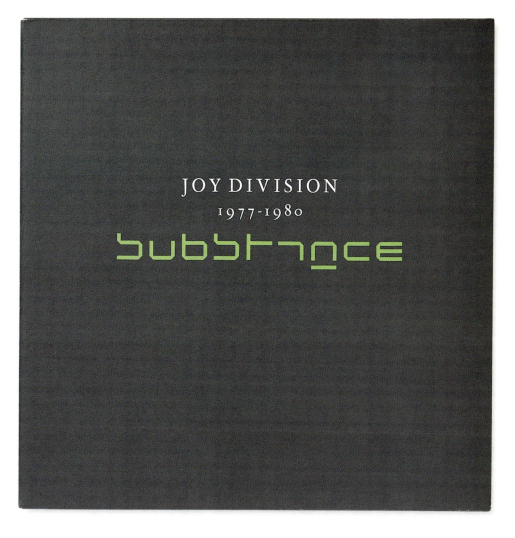

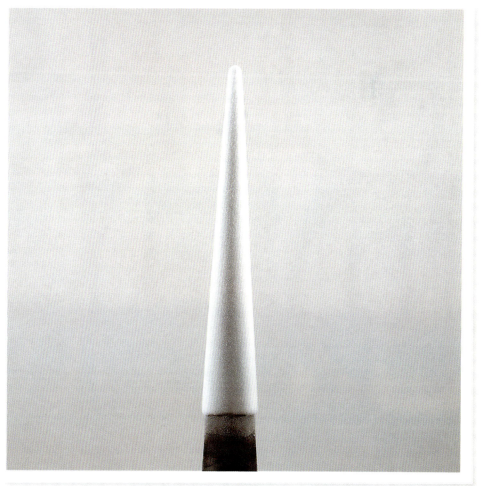

FAC 212

Wrote for Luck marks the arrival of a new dawn for Factory Records. Central Station's free-flowing rhetoric and disregard for formal graphic concerns was unlike anything the label had ever experienced. Although the designers had been involved with Factory since 1985, this release marks a dynamic new sensibility in both graphic and musical terms. Their stream-of-consciousness-like rendering became a signifier of Factory's renaissance. The hand-drawn lettering was an intentional move away from designers relying on type specimen books. However, loose and free as the design is, Central Station clearly understood the power of marketing – they wanted people to be able to spot a Happy Mondays cover from 50 yards.

ARTWORKS – CENTRAL STATION DESIGN

This vivid cover features a tightly cropped portrait of lead singer Shaun Ryder. The dynamic colours and painting technique combine to create a startling image, capturing the hedonistic pleasures of the period. The viewer cannot help but be caught by the haunting, mesmerizing, enormity of the image. Central Station's unique method of image making was later developed across a series of portraits of British entertainers exhibited as the 'Hello Playmates' show in 1990. Artist and title information is blind embossed on the bottom left-hand side of the sleeve, in order to avoid overloading the image with text; the inner sleeve, meanwhile, featured an image of a naked woman and was designed for humour's sake rather than shock value. This image, described by Tony Wilson as 'one of the most profoundly disturbing inner sleeves in record history', left an indelible mark on many.

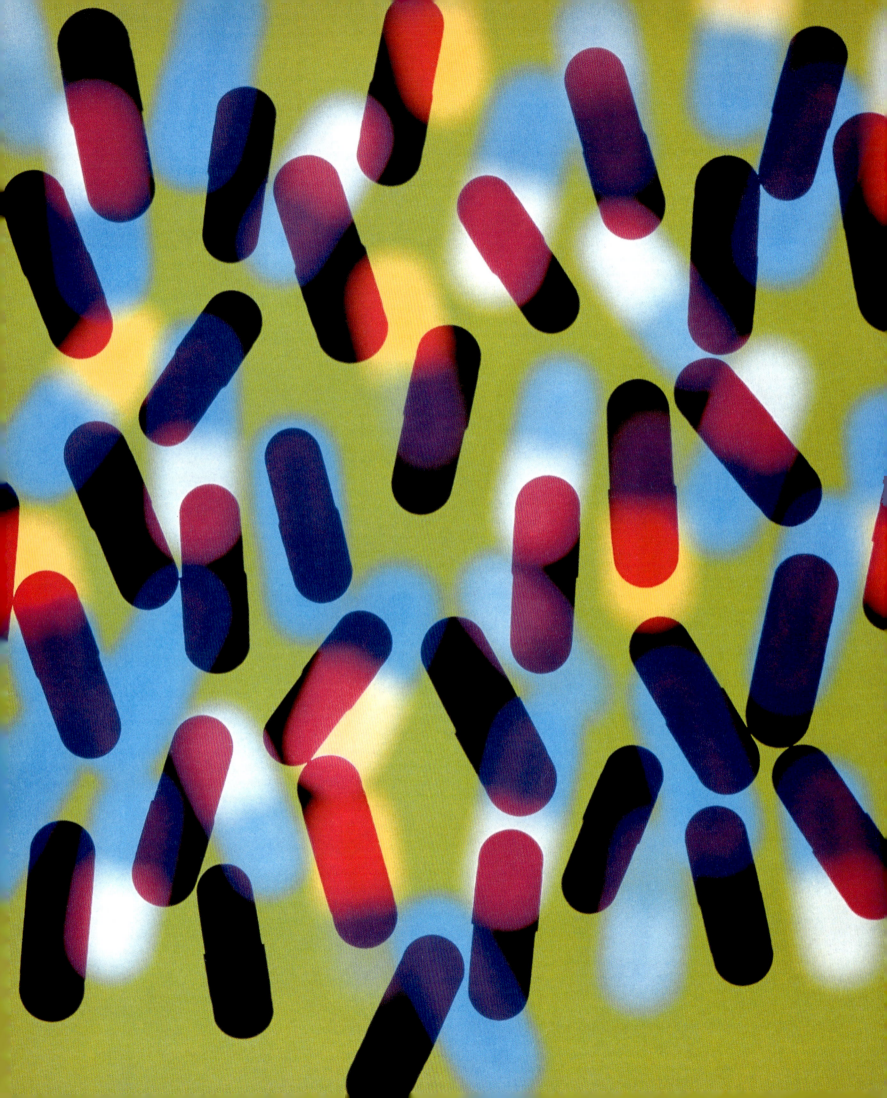

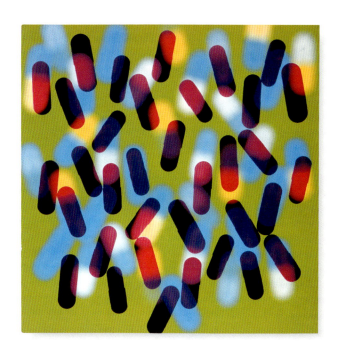

Fine Time captures the spirit of the drug-fuelled club nights of 1988, the hey-day of acid house, which had heavily influenced this album. Based on a painting by Richard Bernstein (1932–2002), the sleeve was generated using Key and Saville's dichromat technique. Pharmaceuticals appeared in different patterns across each format. Saville stated that this was 'the first time a New Order cover reflected something that was actually going on in youth culture'.

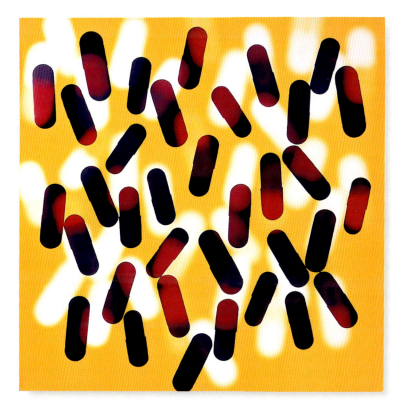

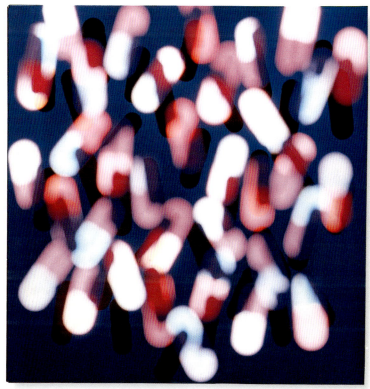

Fac 223 & 223R New Order *Fine Time* / 7-inch, 12-inch & 12-inch remix / 1988 / Des: PSA / Dichromat: Trevor Key & Peter Saville

Fact 275 New Order *Technique* / LP / 1989 / Des: PSA / Dichromat: Trevor Key & Peter Saville

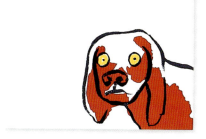

The film clip for Fac 73R (see p. 133) featured the work of US animator Robert Breer and photographer/film-maker William Wegman.
For Christmas 1988 the label produced a facsimile of Breer's flick-book that featured in the clip, signed by Tony Wilson and other key Factory staff on the back cover. Typically for Factory, they went to great – some might say ridiculous – expense, specifying at least six spot colours in addition to four-colour printing for the front cover.

Fac 235 *Christmas Present* / Flick-book / 1988 / Des: PSA /
Illustration: Robert Breer

Fac 263R & 263 New Order *Round & Round* / 12-inch remix & 12-inch / 1989 / Des: PSA /
Dichromat: Trevor Key & Peter Saville
Fac 263DJ New Order *Round & Round* / 12-inch / 1989 / Des: PSA

Fac 263 New Order Round & Round / 7-inch / 1989 / Des: PSA / Dichromat: Trevor Key & Peter Saville

The single *Round & Round* and the LP *Technique* (see p. 148) both feature psychedelic renderings of classical sculptures. Generated using the dichromat technique, the numerous colour combinations evoke the silk-screen multiples of Andy Warhol, while the choice of the antique cherub and bust of Louis XIV was Saville's response to the late 1980s ephemeral commoditization of design culture. These figurative elements are also symbolic of the excesses that would characterize rave culture – the bacchanalian cherub and the Sun King – even if this was not a conscious statement on the designers' part.

THE DURUTTI COLUMN VINI REILLY FACT 244

Fact 244 The Durutti Column *Vini Reilly* / LP / 1989 / Des: Johnson Panas / Ph: Mark Warner

Fact 244

Vini Reilly

The final version of this sleeve, based on the cover of Bob Dylan's *Highway 61 Revisited*, features a black-and-white portrait of central Durutti Column figure Vini Reilly. This design was based on conventional cover art with the image of the performer amplified on the cover and liner notes on the reverse. In order to maintain some authenticity the text on the back was composed using traditional letterpress printing. However, this came after Reilly had rejected an original proposal from 8vo, which had placed greater emphasis on typographic form and played down the commissioned portrait. The third image is the back cover of this initially proposed sleeve.

Fact 244 The Durutti Column *Vini Reilly* / LP proposal / 1989 / Des: 8vo / Ph: Mark Warner

Fact 260 Happy Mondays *Hallelujah* / 12-inch / 1989 / Des: Central Station Design
Fact 217 To Hell with Burgundy *Earthbound* / LP / 1989 / Des: Central Station Design

Happy Mondays and Karl Denver

Here Central Station Design create another alternative to orthodox typography. This bright arrangement is also bloated and sluggish and is delivered in a hallucinogenic daze. The positively slurred speech of the lettering, incorporated into a three-dimensional typographic sculpture through which runs, a river of ink, is the perfect visual accompaniment to the music of *Lazyitis*. Contrast this direct relation between imagery and content with the more suggestive use of a dead fly to subvert the pastoral sleeve of Fact 217 (opposite).

Haçienda Anniversary
seven
may **20** **'89** **/21**

Fac 51 *Haçienda Seventh Anniversary / Poster / 1989 / Des: 8vo*

Facd 219 Kalima *Flyaway* / CD / 1989 / Des: Johnson Panas / Ph: James Martin
Fac 231 *Yo John* Music Week / Advertisement / 1989 / Des: Johnson Panas

Yo John

Fac 231

The seventh birthday poster for The Haçienda opposite is one of the most iconic in the series. Designed by 8vo in 1989, it was constructed by hand at its intended size (1524 x 1016mm), allowing the team to assess the poster's functionality in situ, using a wall on the street near their studio to prototype ideas. Given the large scale of the artwork it then had to be recreated at a reduced scale to fit within the parameters of standard print reprographic equipment. The multi-layered structure combines fluorescent, luminescent and metallic inks, allowing the poster to work during both day and night.

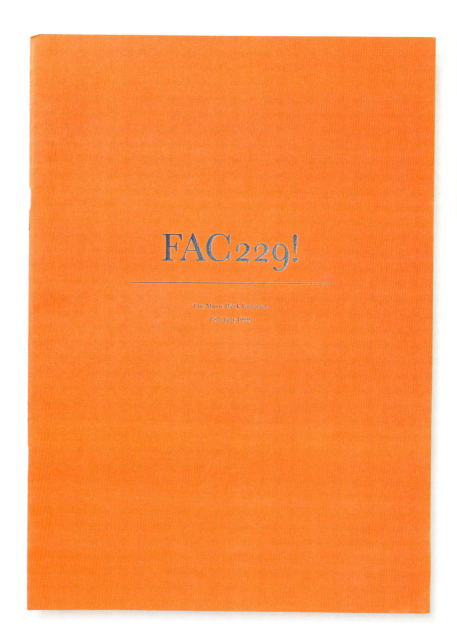

FAC 229!

The Music Week Factorial

15th July 1989

Fac 229 *The Music Week Factorial* / Advertorial Publication / 1989 / Des: PSA

Dave.

MASTER ✳

DRY/201

226×2   60   3144

In 1989 Factory invested in its second built project, a bar situated in Oldham Street, Manchester. Ben Kelly Design (who had been responsible for The Haçienda) were commissioned to create a continental-style bar in the former furniture warehouse. Wilson stated that it would 'be to bars what The Haçienda is to clubs'. This space had a very different purpose to The Haçienda, focusing on the bar-café culture found in places like Barcelona and Los Angeles. As with the Haçienda, it was one of the first of its kind in England, and began a trend. The design of Dry proved to be a worthy complement to the club, offering a different experience though linked by a shared sensibility. Among the mix of rich colours and materials, including concrete, slate, steel, terrazzo and Kelly's signature glazed tiles on the exterior, a range of recycled and found materials were incorporated, including reclaimed telegraph poles. A huge spear-like feature, suspended from the ceiling, ran the length of the bar protruding from the front and rear of the premises from Oldham Street to Spear Street. Many of the original features of the warehouse were saved including a red plaster curtain that became a unique feature of the bar – a trace element of the site's past. Originally conceived to operate over three storeys with a restaurant and gallery on the top, in the end finances limited the project to a bar on the ground floor with the lower ground floor for amenities and storage. The logo was formulated by Johnson Panas, based on elements supplied by Brett Wickens at PSA, and adapted for a range of printed materials including drink mats, serviettes and doggy bags. The promotional poster (p. 163), also designed by Johnson Panas, features overlaid working sketches of various features of the building's design, which included custom beer taps.

Fac 201 Dry / Invitation / 1989 / Des: Johnson Panas

Invitation
Sunday July 23rd 1989
7.00 – 10.30pm

DRY*201*

Opens its doors

Factory Communications' and New Order's
new bar for Manchester
28/30 Oldham Street
Come to the party
This invitation admits two

Dry is designed by Ben Kelly Design

Fac 201 Dry / 1989 / Des: Ben Kelly Design

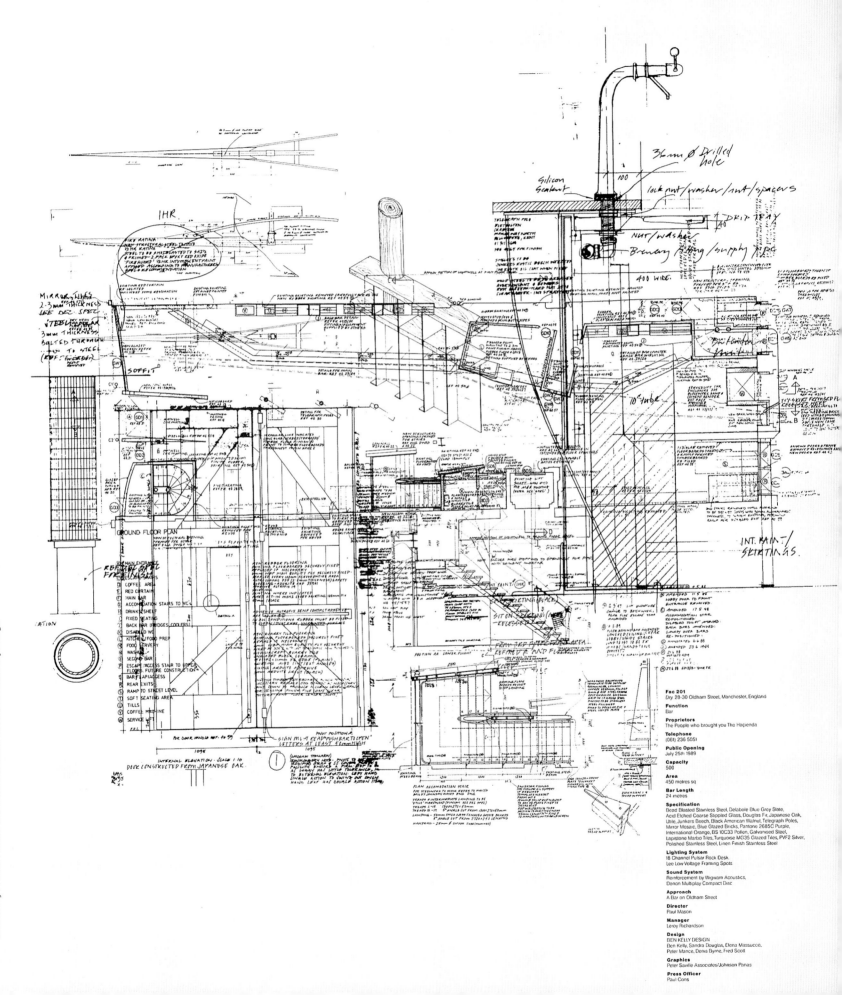

DRY201

Fac 201 Dry / Poster / 1989 / Des: Johnson Panas / Illustration: Ben Kelly Design

Fac 201
Dry: 28-30 Oldham Street, Manchester, England

Function
Bar

Proprietors
The People who brought you The Haçienda

Telephone
(061) 236 5051

Public Opening
July 25th 1989

Capacity
500

Area
450 metres sq

Bar Length
24 metres

Specification
Bead Blasted Stainless Steel, Delabole Blue Grey Slate,
Acid Etched Coarse Stippled Glass, Douglas Fir, Japanese Oak,
Utile, Junkers Beech, Black American Walnut, Telegraph Poles,
Mirror Mosaic, Blue Glazed Bricks, Pantone 2685C Purple,
International Orange, BS 10C33 Pollen, Galvanised Steel,
Lapstone Marble Tiles, Turquoise MG35 Glazed Tiles, PVF2 Silver,
Polished Stainless Steel, Linen Finish Stainless Steel

Lighting System
18 Channel Pulsar Rock Desk.
Lee Low Voltage Framing Spots

Sound System
Reinforcement by Wigwam Acoustics,
Denon Multiplay Compact Disc

Approach
A Bar on Oldham Street

Director
Paul Mason

Manager
Leroy Richardson

Design
BEN KELLY DESIGN
Ben Kelly, Sandra Douglas, Elena Massucco,
Peter Mance, Denis Byrne, Fred Scott

Graphics
Peter Saville Associates/Johnson Panas

Press Officer
Paul Cons

Based on the packaging of Bold detergent, the third single from the *Technique* album is a departure from the dichromat images used on the preceding singles. This purely typographic sleeve is another nod towards Pop Art in its appropriation and reworking of consumer goods. The ironic twist is that the release became embroiled in legal action over the recording's similarity to John Denver's *Leaving on a Jet Plane*.

Fac 273 New Order *Run 2* / 12-inch / 1989 / Des: PSA after Bold

Facd 276

1. **Kreisler String Orchestra:** *Bourrée Classique* — 1:23
   From *Benjamin Britten: Variations on a Theme of Frank Bridge.* Fact 226
   Published by Hawkes & Son Ltd.
2. **Steve Martland:** *Section Four* — 4:59
   From *Drill* by Steve Martland. Fact 266
   Published by Schott & Co. Ltd.
3. **Duke String Quartet:** *2nd Movement (Andante)* — 3:38
   From *String Quartet No. 3* by Michael Tippett. Fact 246
   Published by Schott & Co. Ltd.
4. **Rolf Hind:** *Study No. 6* — 4:06
   Antoine A Varsoise by György Ligeti. Fact 256
   Published by Schott & Co. Ltd.
5. **Robin Williams, Julian Kelly:** *Excerpt from Prelude and Variations* — 5:51
   By Lalliet. Fact 236
   Published by Nova Music Ltd.

A Factory Compact Disc. © 1989 Factory Communications Ltd.
Design Peter Saville Associates

factory
classical 276
label

Facd 276

Factory Classical Label

A Factory Compact Disc

Not for sale. *For promotional use only.*

In 1989 Factory launched its classical music imprint, which was to have its own distinctive house style within the catalogue. Saville looked at classical labels Deutsche Grammophon and ECM for the visual codes and packaging of this genre. There was a conscious desire to package the classical artists in a contemporary fashion that placed emphasis on the performers. PSA established the template for the series, including the specification for extensive liner notes. Tony Wilson approached four other designers to art direct the photography, making each sleeve unique within the context of the brand. Another subtle differentiation was the specification of five dissimilar tints of black ink for the back covers of each. These were printed as spot colours.

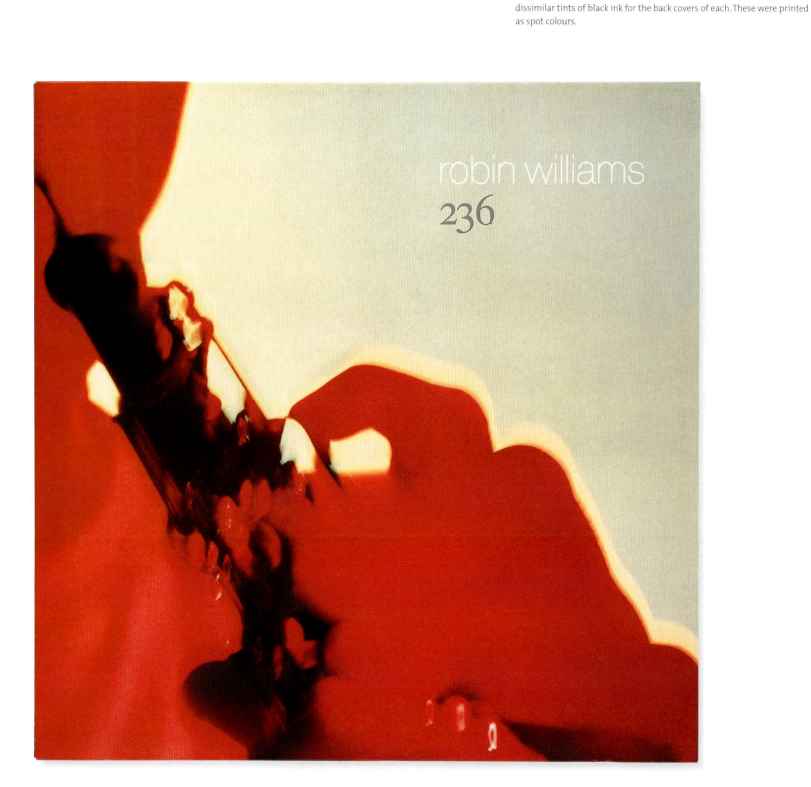

robin williams
236

Fact 236 Robin Williams *Oboe and Piano* / LP / 1989 / Des: PSA / Ph: Phil Cawley / Ph Art Direction: Trevor Johnson for Johnson Panas

Fact 226 Kreisler String Orchestra / LP / 1989 / Des: PSA / Ph: Trevor Key / Ph Art Direction: Peter Saville
Fact 246 Duke String Quartet / LP / 1989 / Des: PSA / Ph: Robert Shackleton / Ph Art Direction: Mark Farrow for 3A

Fact 256 Rolf Hind / LP / 1989 / Des: PSA / Ph: Mark Osborne / Ph Art Direction: Bracken Harper for So What Art Ltd.
Fact 266 Steve Martland / LP / 1989 / Des: PSA / Ph: Andrew Catlin / Ph Art Direction: Neville Brody

Central Station designed a new sleeve for the remix version of this single. The hand-lettered name of the band becomes the backdrop for what appears to be a fish tank. Luminous marine life swimming in the foreground adds a playful dimension to their pre-existing aesthetic. The designers continue to construct uniquely amusing and immediate visual forms in a loose and expressive manner that fits the music perfectly.

Fac 232 Happy Mondays *Wrote for Luck* / 12-inch / 1989 / Des: Central Station Design

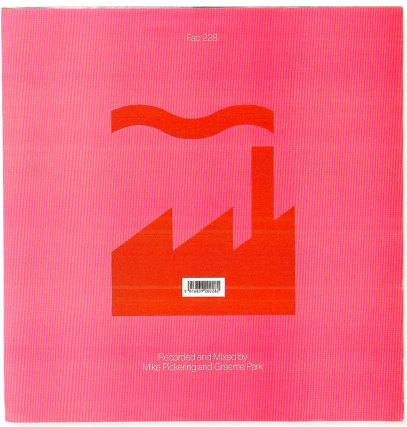

Fac 228 Karl Denver *Wimoweh* 89 / 12-inch / 1989 / Des: Johnson Panas

HAPPY MONDAYS

MADCHESTER

MADCHESTER ®

RAVE ON

E.P.

'Madchester' became the unofficial name of the city during the height of its musical renaissance of the late 1980s. The success of Happy Mondays and non-Factory bands such as The Stone Roses, as well as the reinvigorated Haçienda, all combined to reposition the city as a pop-cultural centre. Central Station Design developed a cartoon-like logotype suggestive of the logos of animators Hanna-Barbera and DC Comics superhero Batman. This appropriation of such motifs suited the period, which in the designers' experience was unreal and akin to 'a cartoon lifestyle with a dark undercurrent'. The logo came in a range of colour combinations and became a key signifier of this historic moment.

Central Station Design studio / Manchester / 1989

REVENGE

Electromix

Fac 247 *Revenge Seven Reasons* / 12-inch / 1989 / Des: PSA / Ph: Trevor Watson
Fac 257R *Electronic Getting Away With It* / 12-inch / 1989 / Des: PSA

"Getting away with it... Electronic!"

Fac 257 Electronic *Getting Away With It* / 12-inch / 1989 / Des: PSA

For Electronic's debut single PSA used stock photography for the first time. This cover employs the visual language of modern print advertising with the title and band name positioned as a caption would appear. The overall design is suggestive of the advertisements and lifestyle pages found in men's magazines such as *Playboy* during the 1970s and 80s. The implied sophistication is interesting given the nature of the act as a highly marketable 'supergroup' consisting of members of New Order, The Smiths and the Pet Shop Boys – all seminal 80s acts. The remix uses a negative version of the key image with the title based on the Panasonic logotype.

Fac 51
The Haçienda
England
1989

Now Available

New T-Shirts
Orange/Blue + Green/Pink

Long Sleeved £12·50
Short Sleeved £7·50

Available From:
Fac 51 **The Haçienda**
11–13 Whitworth Street West Manchester M1 5WG
061 236 5051

*«the absence of the object
becomes a presence you can feel»*

281

artefacts, tee-shirts, posters and trivia
from factory communications limited,
fac 51 the haçienda and dry 201

2nd floor, affleck's arcade, manchester

the area FAC 281

Fac 245 *Christmas Present* / Postcard Set / 1989 / Des: Johnson Panas

Factory's Christmas gift for 1989 was a set of five perforated concertina
postcards. Each card featured a photograph of a Manchester landmark,
hand retouched to read 'Madchester', playing on the upsurge of optimism
that the city was experiencing. The cards were housed in a self-covering
envelope printed in metallic ink.

A good example of Factory's lack of business acumen was its refusal to make contractual agreements with any of the artists. However, towards the end of its life, the label eventually adopted contracts, and typically decided to make a design statement in the process. 8vo developed custom binders that sandwiched contracts between two twelve-inch-square sheets of screen-printed Perspex. These were fastened together by three large industrial bolts, designed to prevent easy consultation. On the covering page of the contract Factory insisted on using an explicit sadomasochistic image – a pun on the label having the artist by the proverbials.

Fac 221 *Factory Contract* / Binder / 1990 / Des: 8vo

This commission coincided with the first commercial use of the Apple Macintosh desktop computer by 8vo. The designers took the opportunity to experiment with the computer's typographic capabilities: tasks that would have once been extremely time-consuming were now immediate. 8vo, like designers across the world, could arrive at solutions sooner than ever before imagined. Here the team continue to push the boundaries of typographic communication while demonstrating an ability to create with a reduced font and colour palette.

Kalima : Shine

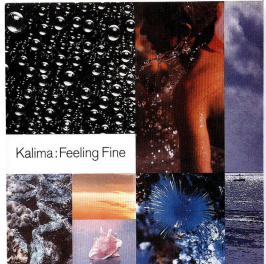

Kalima : Feeling Fine

Fac 269 Kalima *Shine* / 12-inch / 1990 / Des: Johnson Panas
Fact 249 Kalima *Feeling Fine* / LP / 1990 / Des: Johnson Panas

Fac Off

Fac 258 *Fac Off* / T-shirt design / 1990 / Des: Central Station Design

New Factory act Northside very much carried the then defining sound of the scene influenced by bands such as Happy Mondays and The Stone Roses – Central Station were the obvious choice for the sleeve. 'Northside' is rendered in an informal cartoon-like manner, with the central motifs of both this and the following single being pieces of fruit. The references to drugs in the lyrics of this single are explicit and this is reflected in the vivid colour palette derived from housing corporation paint. Central Station demonstrate the ability to maintain a bold identity while customizing each release through the application of various colours and textures.

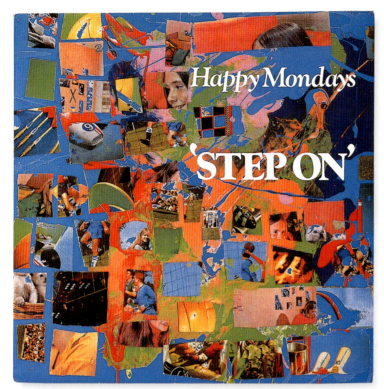

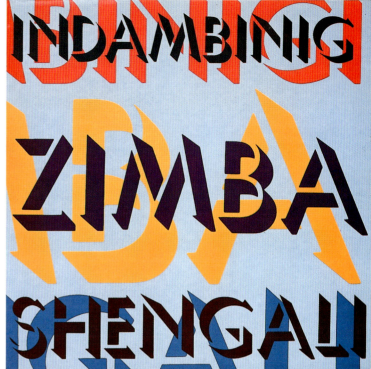

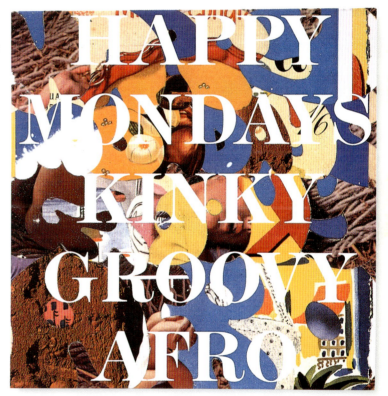

Fac 272 Happy Mondays *Step On* / 12-inch / 1990 / Des: Central Station Design
Fac 298 Northside *My Rising Star* / 12-inch / 1990 / Des: Central Station Design

Fac 278 Indambinig *Zimbi* / 12-inch / 1990 / Des: Central Station Design
Fac 302 Happy Mondays *Kinky Afro* / 12-inch / 1990 / Des: Central Station Design

The United States of the Hacienda

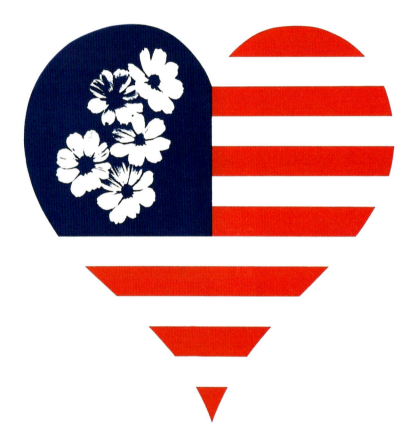

Manchester in New York

New York 14-18 July 1990
'Soundfactory' 542 West 27th Street New York

Featuring
Happy Mondays, 808 State, Adamski, Northside
DJ's: Mike Pickering, Graeme Park, Paul Oakenfold

For further details/Travel information contact:
Fac 51 The Hacienda 061 236 5051
or pick up a fact-sheet from club reception

Fac 51 Manchester England 1990

Fac 51 *The United States of the Hacienda* / Flyer / 1990 / Des: Johnson Panas

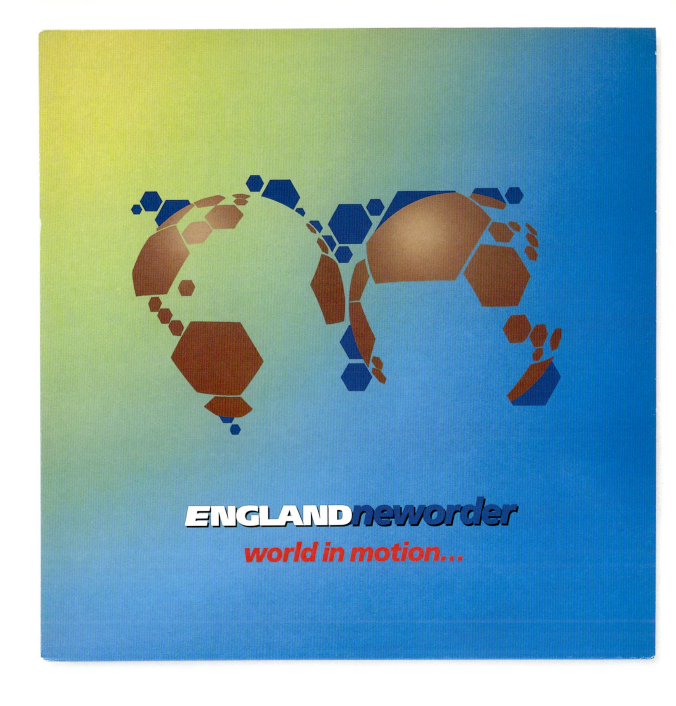

'World in Motion' was the official theme song of the English football team for the 1990 FIFA World Cup, and as such was the first significant mainstream commercial success for the band. PSA developed an iconic sleeve that symbolized football as the world's game by redefining the continents of the globe as the hexagonal panels of a football. The designers were shocked that it had not been done before, despite its striking simplicity, and soon realized that the motif could transcend its original commission and have real potential in the then burgeoning sports merchandise market. However, disagreements between Factory and the designers over the copyright meant that it never went any further than small-scale promotional material for the single.

Fac 293R EnglandNewOrder *World in Motion* / 12-inch / 1990 / Des: PSA

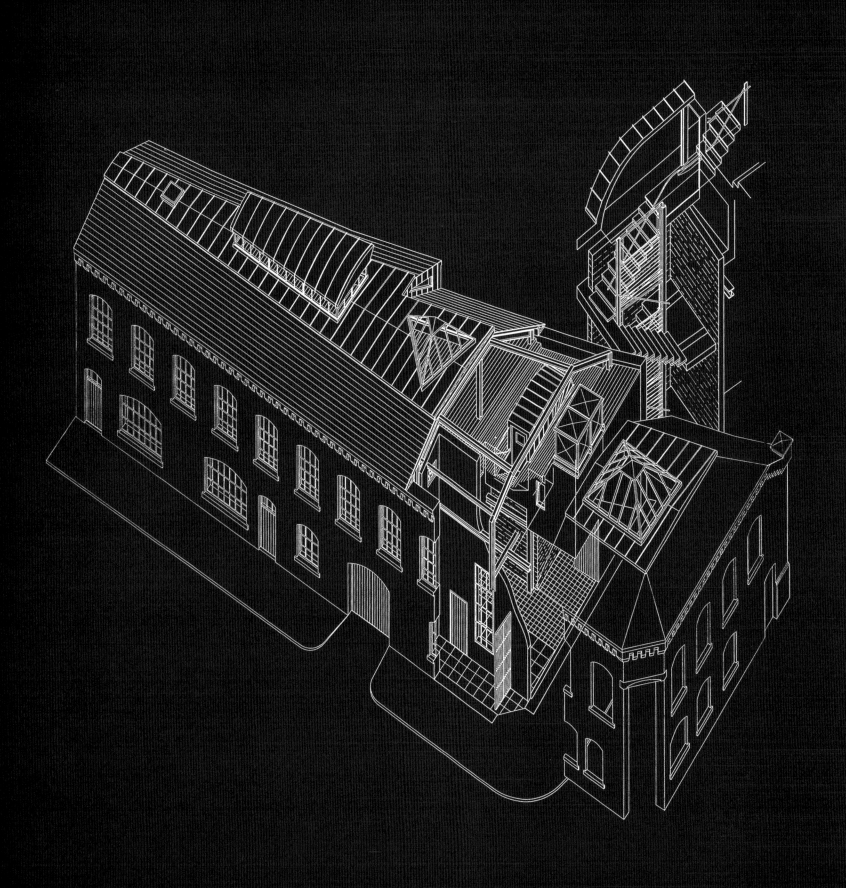

In 1988 Factory purchased a disused textile warehouse in the city centre as its new headquarters. This three-storey building was a major leap up from Alan Erasmus's one-bedroom flat, from which Factory had been run since the late 1970s. Ben Kelly Design was commissioned to rework the space, their third and final built project for the label. As with the preceding projects the designers took an existing shell and redefined the interior space. Though not a public space like The Haçienda or Dry, the Charles Street HQ nevertheless had to be a grand statement for the label as it increasingly positioned itself as a corporate entity. Entrance to the building was through two large steel gates (featuring a perforated plaque of the Factory logo – see p. 184), into a large opening cut through all three floors of the building. The path from reception on the ground floor to the boardroom in the roof space featured brilliantly coloured walls, exposed brickwork and recycled wood panelling; skirting boards were troughs filled with sea-washed pebbles. The overall design was restrained compared to the tasteful flamboyance of Facs 51 and 201, due both to financial limitations and to its function as a workspace. The new HQ would become the home of all Factory operations including the label and leisure activities – Dry and Haçienda. The in-house design studio operated from the basement. However, the purchase and renovation of this building would be a contributing factor to the label's collapse in 1992. If The Haçienda was a three-dimensional manifestation of the Factory aesthetic, Fac 251 was a mausoleum to the corporate brand that the label could never be.

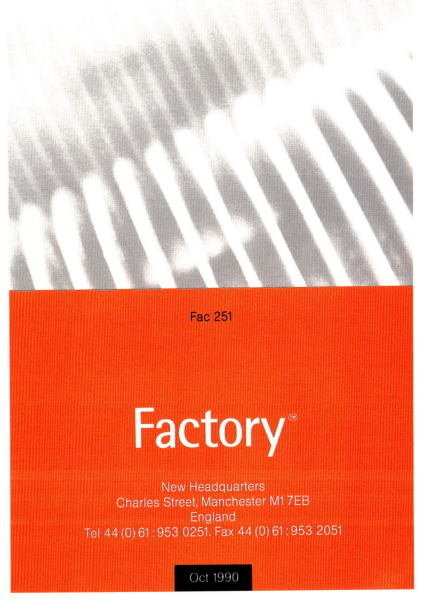

Fac 251

Factory™

New Headquarters
Charles Street, Manchester M1 7EB
England
Tel 44 (0) 61 : 953 0251. Fax 44 (0) 61 : 953 2051

Oct 1990

Fac 251 New Factory HQ / Axonometric drawing / *c.* 1989 / Des: Ben Kelly Design
Fac 251 New Factory HQ / Entrance and interior / 1990 / Des: Ben Kelly Design
Fac 251 New Factory HQ / Postcard / 1990 / Des: Johnson Panas

Factory

The final Factory logo was designed to coincide with the company's relocation to Charles Street in late 1990. The new identity marked a departure from the label's industrial past in favour of becoming an elegant and futuristic brand. The corporate font, Factis 90, was a reworking of Otl Aicher's Rotis. Guidelines were developed for its application to all releases, the first time a house style had been imposed at Factory. This was very much influenced by the corporate approach that Saville and Brett Wickens were witnessing during their time at Pentagram. Former PSA employee Julian Morey was responsible for the creation of the Factory stationery, including the letterhead, continuation sheet, envelope and compliments slip, each printed in different metallic inks. The label was still prepared to indulge in the details.

Factory Communications Ltd. / Logo / 1990 / Des: PSA

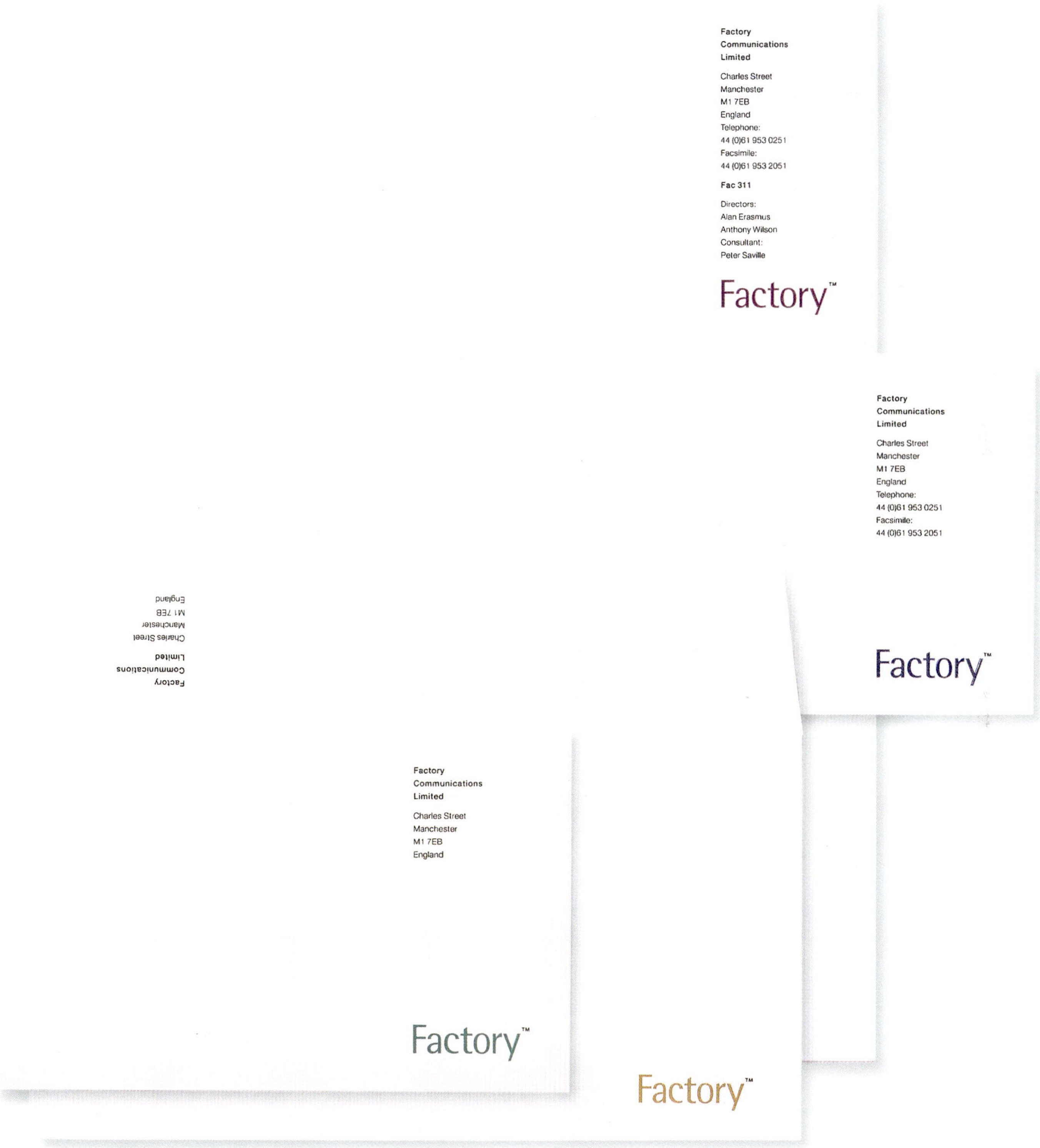

Factory
Communications
Limited

Charles Street
Manchester
M1 7EB
England
Telephone:
44 (0)61 953 0251
Facsimile:
44 (0)61 953 2051

Fac 311

Directors:
Alan Erasmus
Anthony Wilson
Consultant:
Peter Saville

Factory™

Factory
Communications
Limited

Charles Street
Manchester
M1 7EB
England
Telephone:
44 (0)61 953 0251
Facsimile:
44 (0)61 953 2051

Factory™

Factory
Communications
Limited

Charles Street
Manchester
M1 7EB
England

Factory
Communications
Limited

Charles Street
Manchester
M1 7EB
England

Factory™

Factory™

Fac 311 *Fourth Generation Stationery* / 1990 / Des: Julian Morey

REVENGE ONE TRUE PASSION
SIDE A PINEAPPLE FACE
BIG BANG KISS THE CHROME
SLAVE SIDE B BLEACHMAN
SURF NAZI FAG HAG IT'S QUIET

Produced and recorded by REVENGE at Suite 16 Studio, Rochdale, Manchester, England. Engineered by Michael Johnson.
Mixed by Alan Meyerson at Larrabee Sound using the B.A.S.E. REVENGE are Peter Hook - bass, keyboards & vocals.
Dave Hicks - guitar, keyboards & backing vocals, Chris Jones - keyboards.

Art Direction by Peter Saville. REVENGE girl Joanne photographed by Suze Randall. Special thanks to David Hinds.
Styling by Donna Bertolino. Hair and make up by Alexis Vogel. Jewellery courtesy of Leparesca L.A. Design by PSA London.

Factory™

A Factory Record · 1990 Factory Communications Ltd

Revenge was the solo project for Peter Hook of New Order. This artwork adopts the aesthetics of fetish/glamour photography. This overtly sexual image is in stark contrast to much of New Order's visual representation. Peter Saville commissioned former *Penthouse* and *Hustler* photographer Suze Randall to create the images. These photographs utilize the then taboo visual vocabulary of pornography, recontextualizing it within record design at a time when allusions to the porn industry were not as chic as they are today.

Fact 230 Revenge *One True Passion* / LP / 1990 / Des: PSA / Ph: Suze Randall
Fac 267 Revenge *Pineapple Face* / 12-inch / 1990 / Des: PSA / Ph: Suze Randall

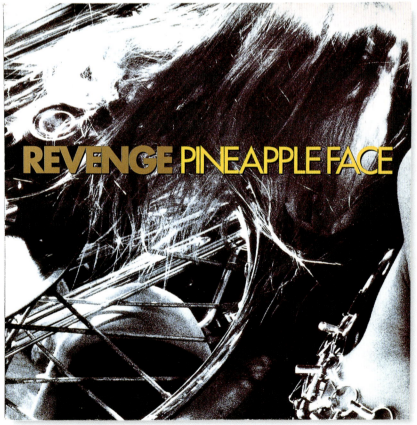

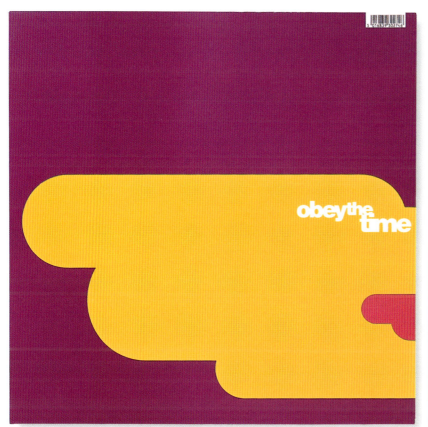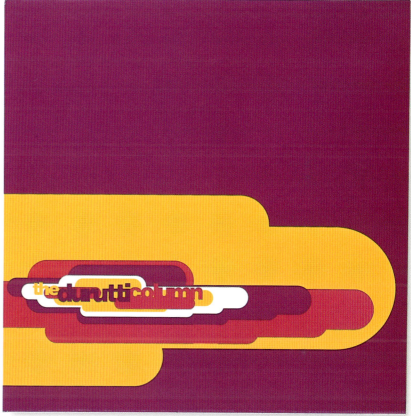

8vo continued their experimentation with computers, this time exploring shapes that would have been difficult to execute using pre-digital tools such as pens and compasses. The designers had a very restricted font palette, namely the Helvetica family, and yet set about manipulating this default font to create something new. The colour palette is very much of its period, though this was unintentional on the designers' part.

Fact 274 The Durutti Column *Obey The Time* / LP / 1990 / Des: 8vo

Fact 320 Happy Mondays *Pills 'N' Thrills and Bellyaches* / LP / 1990 / Des: Central Station Design

Pills 'N' Thrills... (originally to be titled *Kinky Album*) was a transatlantic production, recorded in Los Angeles and mixed in London. The designers wanted visually to represent this exchange by combining ephemera from both cities. Factory agreed to finance a trip to America enabling Central Station to collect a variety of material, spending a week in Los Angeles with the band when they were recording the album. This material was used inside the typography while the English equivalent was used as a background. This originally released version can be seen opposite, and below left and right (front cover, back cover and insert respectively). Such a resourceful use of printed matter is typical of the output of Central Station Design, and reflects their life-long compulsion to collect all sorts of printed ephemera. However, when the album came to be released in the US, fear of legal action for copyright infringement led to a redesign (above, right).

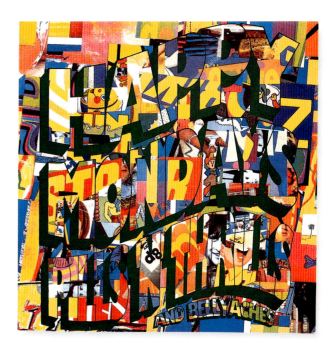

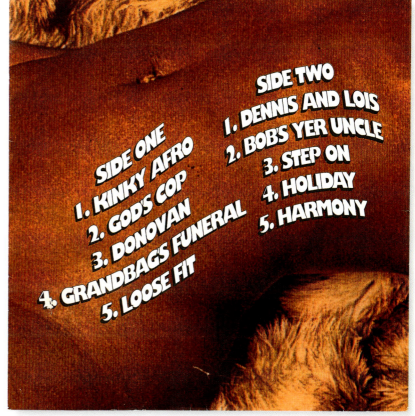

Xmas Greetings from Factory – Dec 1990

Fac 295 *Christmas Present* / Photo Print / 1990 / Des: Uncredited / Ph: Julie Phipps

Johnson Panas's sleeve for Electronic's eponymous debut LP is a
signification of the band's name. A line screen placed over a composite
portrait of the band simulates their appearance on a computer display,
while the logotype and track listing, both hand rendered, are based
on digital alphabets designed by Dutch typographer Wim Crouwel.
International orange was selected as the primary colour in keeping with its
use on all promotional material for Factory's new headquarters. Since the
duo consisted of Bernard Sumner of New Order and Johnny Marr of The
Smiths (with help from the Pet Shop Boys), it was important to project an
image that did not overlap with their usual bands' graphic identities.

316   I Fagiolini

The Art of Monteverdi

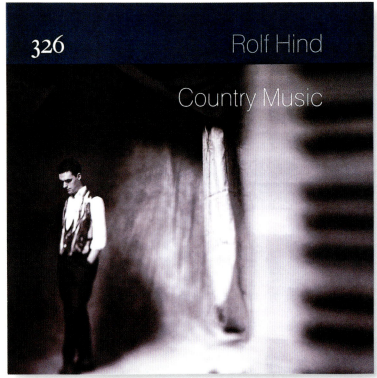

326   Rolf Hind

Country Music

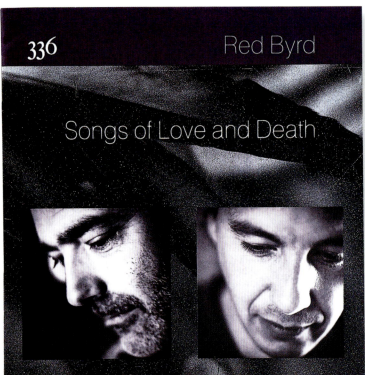

336   Red Byrd

Songs of Love and Death

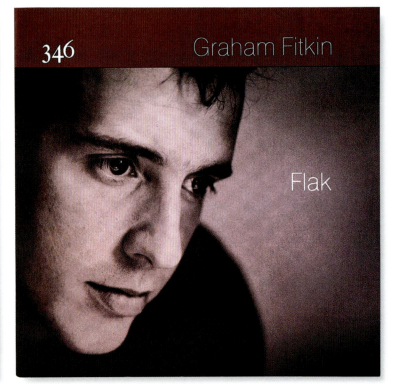

346   Graham Fitkin

Flak

Facd 316 I Fagiolini *The Art of Monteverdi* / CD / 1991 / Des: Bill Smith Studio / Ph: The Douglas Brothers
Facd 326 Rolf Hind *Country Music* / CD / 1991 / Des: Bill Smith Studio / Ph: The Douglas Brothers
Facd 336 Red Byrd *Songs of Love and Death* / CD / 1991 / Des: Bill Smith Studio / Ph: The Douglas Brothers
Facd 346 Graham Fitkin *Flak* / CD / 1991 / Des: Bill Smith Studio / Ph: The Douglas Brothers

Facd 356 Eric Satie *Socrate* / CD / 1991 / Des: Bill Smith Studio / Ph: The Douglas Brothers

356   Eric Satie

ILFO

0578

Socrate

Bill Smith Studio was commissioned to design and coordinate the second generation of Factory classical releases in 1990. The designers were to follow the existing format designed by PSA (see p. 166) in terms of typographic style and muted colour palette, but to take it further. This time the Douglas Brothers did all of the photography, leading to more consistent portraiture, as opposed to the varying levels of abstraction in the previous series. However, different techniques were employed to suggest the unique characteristics of each of the performers. Special inks, including metallic inks, were used in the printing.

vinireilly
fac284
aside:
thetogether
mix
bside:
contra-indications
version
rays
(up-personmix)

Fac 284 Vini Reilly (The Durutti Column) *The Together Mix* / 12-inch / 1991 / Des: 8vo

Following on from Fact 274, 8vo set about restricting their palette in order to simplify the message. Departing from densely layered graphic forms and stripping things back to one typeface and two colours, the designers deliver the same primary typographic content on both sides of the sleeve. However, only the information relevant to the side the reader is viewing is actually readable. This positive and negative effect is further enhanced by the inversion of colours.

vinireilly
fac284
aside:
thetogether
mix
bside:
1contra-indications
(albumversion)
2fridays
(up-personmix)

Fac **287** Electronic *Get the Message* / 12-inch / 1991 / Des: Johnson Panas

This second single for Electronic is clearly denoted by the numeral '2'. This modernist, purely typographic resolution is in contrast to the stock photography of the band's previous single (see p. 173), designed by PSA. The visual strength of this sleeve lies in the numerous colour combinations, while maintaining a consistent typographic message. Each format employs two different process colours making each unique. This system was also carried across to overseas releases licensed to other labels. Mark Farrow was commissioned to design the 12-inch remix, which has no relationship to Johnson Panas's sleeve. Here the designer is appropriating the style and iconography of contemporary motor-cross bike racing.

Fac **287** Electronic *Get the Message* / 7-inch / 1991 / Des: Johnson Panas
Fac **287R** Electronic *Get the Message* / 12-inch / 1991 /
Des: Mark Farrow for 3A

This song was among those censored for radio play in the UK during the 1991 Gulf War due to the anti-war sentiment of its lyrics. Although the song itself has a relatively up-tempo feel, delivered in the trademark Happy Mondays sound, there is a very dark and sinister subtext to the track. Central Station Design set about capturing this idea by composing a murkier experience. The burnt fat on the back cover (not shown) to simulate burnt, bubbling human flesh was used to suggest the violence of warfare.

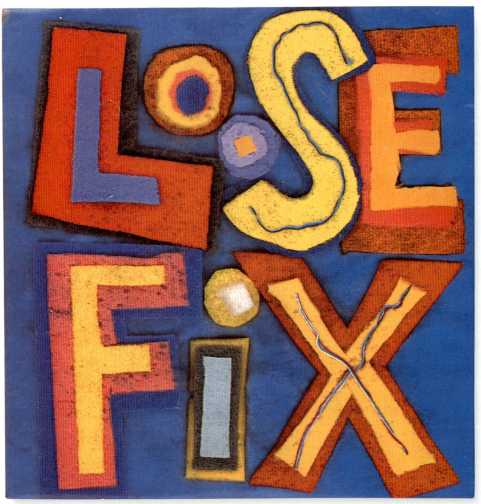

Fac 312 Happy Mondays *Loose Fit* / 12-inch / 1991 / Des: Central Station Design
Fac 312R Happy Mondays *Loose Fix* / 12-inch / 1991 / Des: Central Station Design

Fac 51 *Halluçienda* / Poster / 1991 / Des: Julian Morey / Ph: Science Photo Library

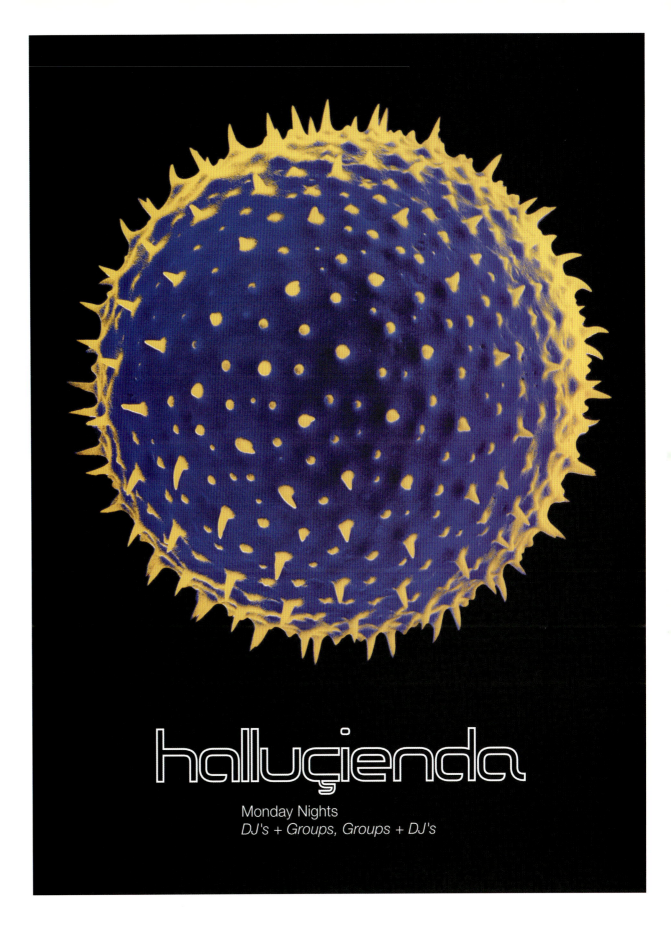

This poster captures the spirit of The Haçienda during its commercial peak in the early 1990s. The wordplay with the name of the club and 'hallucination', combined with a luminescent alien object, captures the hedonism of club culture – modern-day psychedelia. The image is a microscopic photograph of a pollen spore. Its pulsating form, rising from the darkness, is not so far removed from the celestial atmosphere of *Unknown Pleasures* – but in this instance the message is very much alive.

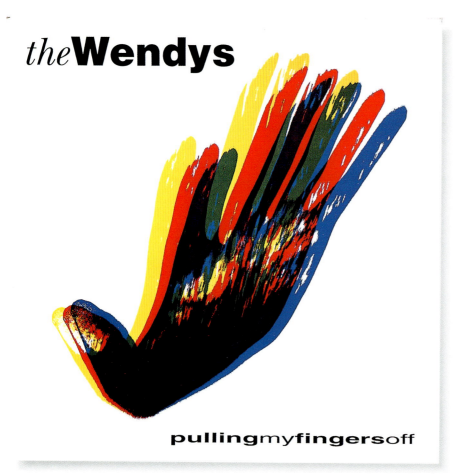

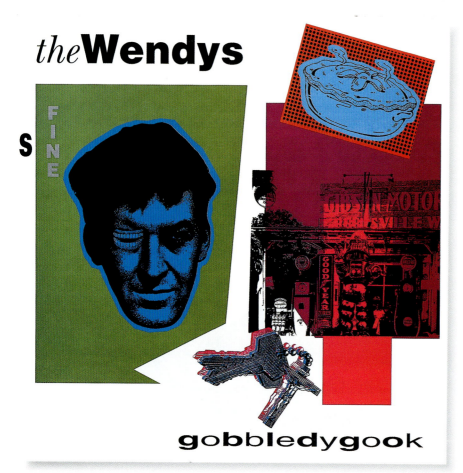

Liverpool-based artist and musician David Knopov was approached to design the artwork for The Wendys in 1991. Factory, again, were marrying an act with an artist. Knopov set about generating an image for each song on the album using his characteristic approach to image-making. Taking inspiration from a single word, sentence or idea from each song, the collages were all produced by hand with the aid of a conventional photocopier. The logotype is based on the masthead of *The Guardian* newspaper (before it changed in 2005).

Fac 297 The Wendys *Pulling My Fingers Off* / 12-inch / 1991 / Des: David Knopov
Fact 285 The Wendys *Gobbledygook* / LP / 1991 / Des: David Knopov /
Ph: Stefan De Batselier

Fact 310 Northside *Chicken Rhythms* / LP / 1991 / Des: Central Station Design

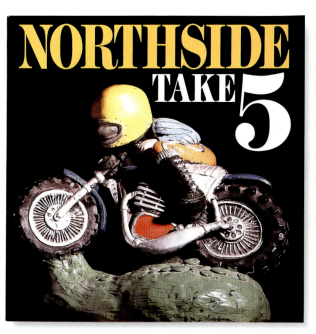

In conveying the more offbeat aspect of Northside, Central Station's handling of their visual projection utilized a 'Pop'-style placement of the band members' smiling faces, suggestive of The Beatles. These were superimposed over Far Eastern commercial graphics of animals playing instruments. The designers wanted to emphasize the funny side of a band, who arguably did not take themselves too seriously. This nostalgic referencing of popular culture and 'Made in China' commercial products places the band within a specific pop ephemera context.

Fac 308 Northside *Take 5* / 12-inch / 1991 / Des: Central Station Design / Ph: Mick Green

8vo's final commission for Factory was designed in response to the preceding birthday poster, of 1990 (see p. 176). Here the designers move away from layered, intricate and computer-driven composition towards a simple and direct typographic statement. The message is succinct and delivered without any visual interference, demonstrating a new restraint and an example of transparent communication that is visually stimulating.

Haçienda Nine
21 May 1991
Fac 51

8vo

cath carroll
ENGLAND MADE ME

Fact 210 Cath Carroll *England Made Me* / LP / 1991 / Des: Chris Mathan / Ph: Julian Broad

In April 1991, record producer and early Factory partner Martin Hannett passed away. Factory released a compilation in memory of his lifetime's work. Hannett not only defined the label's early sound, but was also an extremely influential producer during the post-Punk period. The tranquil sleeve, photographed by Trevor Key, with ripples emanating in a pond, symbolizes his legacy. The typographic detail for the front cover is confined to the vertical sash.

Fact 325 Various Artists *Martin* / LP / 1991 / Des: In-house / Ph: Trevor Key

The work of record producer Martin Hannett

MARTIN

BUZZCOCKS: Breakdown
SLAUGHTER AND THE DOGS:
Cranked Up Really High
JOHN COOPER CLARKE:
Suspended Sentence
JOY DIVISION:
She's Lost Control
JILTED JOHN: Jilted John
A CERTAIN RATIO: Do The Du
ORCHESTRAL MANOEUVRES
IN THE DARK: Almost
U2: 11 O'Clock Tick Tock
NEW ORDER:
Everything's Gone Green
HAPPY MONDAYS: Lazyitis
WORLD OF TWIST:
She's A Rainbow
NEW FAST AUTOMATIC
DAFFODILS: Get Better
THE HIGH: More

Factory

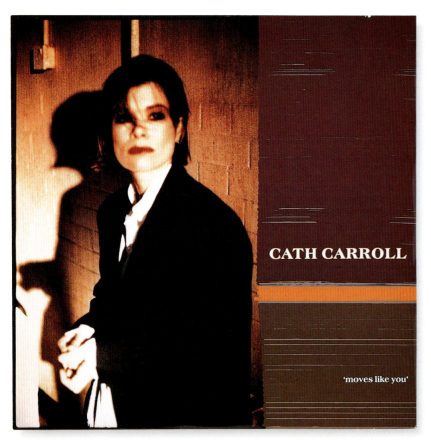

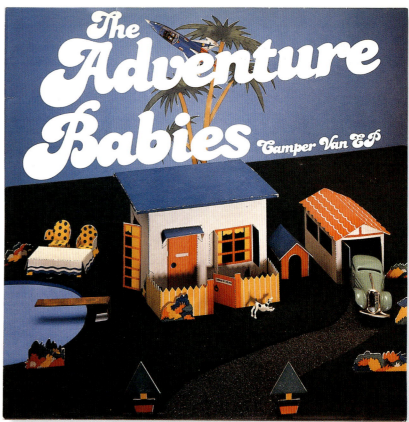

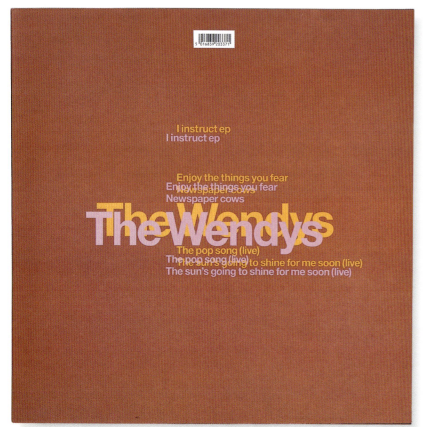

Fac 307 Cath Carroll *Moves Like You* / 12-inch / 1991 / Des: Two / Ph: The Douglas Brothers
Fact 337 The Wendys *I Instruct* / 12-inch / 1991 / Des: In-house

Fac 319 The Adventure Babies *Camper Van* / 12-inch / 1991 / Des: Central Station Design
Fac 329 The Other Two *Tasty Fish* / 12-inch / 1991 / Des: Colin Taylor & Michael Worthington at Studio Dm / Ph: Alan Jones

The intent of Central Station Design was to play with the notion of a 'live' experience for the artwork. Using inanimate mannequin heads, this is a pseudo-live situation, which was in their words 'a live album with a dead head'. Here the designers focus on the photographic content rather than the heavy typography of earlier Happy Mondays sleeves. The subtle lettering is rendered using rubber stamps. Instead of the obligatory design credit on the album, 'Central Station Salon' take responsibility for 'Wigs and Gigs'. There is the usual wicked sense of humour and irony at play.

Fact 322 Happy Mondays *Live* / Double LP / 1991 / Des: Central Station Design / Ph: Mick Green
Following Spread The Other Two / Logo / 1991 / Des: Colin Taylor & Michael Worthington at Studio Dm

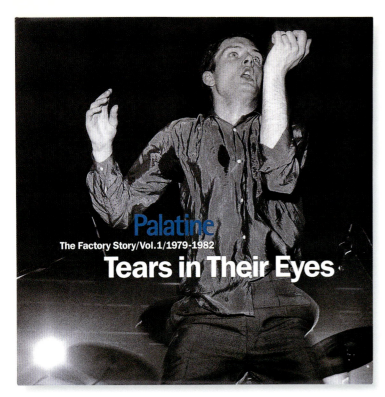

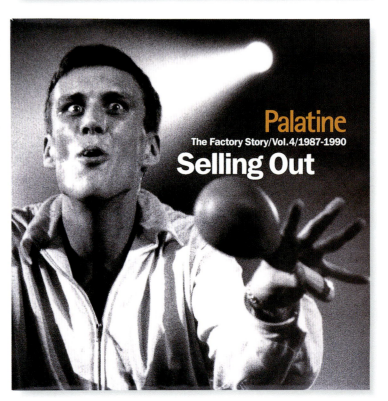

Fact 314, 324, 334 & 344 Various Artists *Palatine – The Factory Story* / LPs / 1991 / Des: In-house / Ph: Kevin Cummins

This Factory retrospective was divided into four thematic chapters: volume 1, *Tears in Their Eyes*, focused on the musical legacy of producer Martin Hannett and Joy Division; volume 2, *Life's A Beach*, surveyed its early 1980s dance experience; volume 3, *The Beat Groups*, celebrated the guitar bands that defined Factory for a period; and volume 4, *Selling Out*, showcased the more recent output on the label, much of which had been commercially successful. These were albums to be sold individually or as a complete boxed set with a 32-page booklet. Black-and-white images were selected from the archive of local photographer Kevin Cummins, who had documented many bands over the years. The title was set in the house font Factis 90 in keeping with the label's new corporate identity. The same box was used for all formats including CD and cassette.

Palatine

The Factory Story/1979-1990

Palatine

The Factory Story/1979-1990

Tears in Their Eyes, Life's A Beach
The Beat Groups, Selling Out

Factory

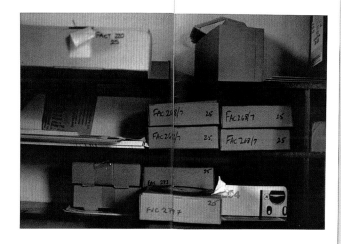

Fact 400 Various Artists *Palatine – The Factory Story* / Box-set & Booklet /
1991 / Des: In-house / Ph: Kevin Cummins, Ged Murray & Peter Walsh

Judge Fudge is a seductively colourful yet toxic miasma of melted plastic toys and lettering. Central Station Design had experimented with the concept of painting with plastic. Through testing the varying melting points, they set out to create a bed of layered materials leaving the typography as the last ingredient. This assemblage was baked in an oven in their office the process taking several hours to resolve. This actual process turned out to be hazardous as the oven door would not shut allowing toxic fumes to fill the air with the designers suffering the consequences. The designers describe this as their 'Hell' – pre-Chapman Brothers.

Factory

5016839203326

FAC 332
Photography Mick Green
Art Central Station Design

electronic *feel every beat* / *remixes*

A. Feel Every Beat. 12" Remix. (6.48). B. Feel Every Beat. Dub Mix. (6.02). Bi. Lean to the Inside. (4.08).
Bernard Sumner: Vocals, keyboards and programming. Johnny Marr: Guitars, keyboards and programming. Thanks to
DNA for additional programming. Written and produced by Bernard Sumner and Johnny Marr. Engineered by Owen Morris.
Recorded at Clear, Manchester. 12" and Dub mix by Danny Rampling and Pete Lorimer. Published by Warner Chappell.
Packaged by 3a. Photograph by Donald Christie. ℗ + © 1991 Factory Communications Ltd. Licensed by Clear Productions Ltd.

Factory

FAC 328

This sleeve is intentionally designed to confuse the viewer. All the
information one would expect on the reverse of a record – track listing,
running times and production credits – are placed on the front. Likewise,
the studio portrait of the band is placed on the back. It was not uncommon
to see the 12-inch vinyl versions incorrectly displayed in stores, and even
repackaged incorrectly overseas. This was less of a problem for the CD
single and cassette versions given their format. The blocks printed in silver
on the cover are based on the DX coding found on 35mm film canisters.

Fac 328 Electronic *Feel Every Beat* / 12-inch / 1991 / Des: Mark Farrow for 3A /
Ph: Donald Christie

The Third Birthday Party

Wednesday 22nd July, 8pm till late.

Guest DJs: Tom Wainwright, John McCready, Stef.

DRY**201**

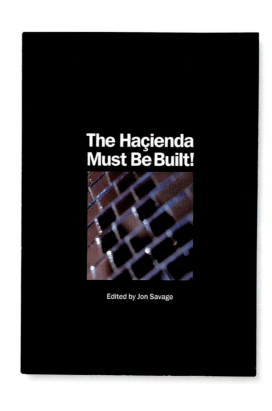

The Haçienda Must Be Built!

Edited by Jon Savage

Fac 201 *The Third Birthday Party* / Ticket / 1992 / Des: In-house
Fac 351 *The Haçienda Must Be Built!* / Book / 1992 / Des: In-house

Gun World Porn

REVENGE

Factory's final classical releases were a departure from the aesthetic that defined the earlier titles. The images are semi-abstract photographs by Bernard Oglesby, moving away from portraits of the artist while maintaining a typographic link. The designer John Macklin took the liner notes further by introducing French and German translations in addition to the English text. On Facd 366 the designer also created a diagrammatic representation of the performance and recording arrangements of the musicians and conductor for each of the five pieces of music on the CD.

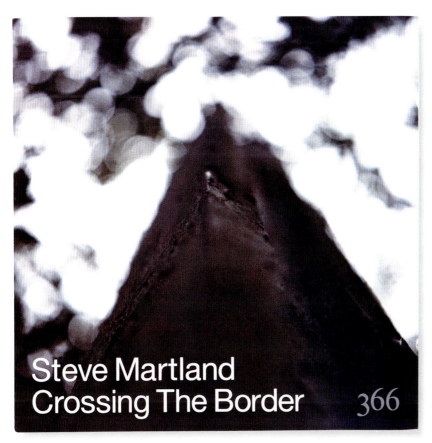

Steve Martland
Crossing The Border 366

Martland plays Mozart

406
Wolfgang

Facd 366 Steve Martland *Crossing the Border* / CD / 1992 / Des: In-house / Ph: Bernard Oglesby

Facd 406 Steve Martland *Wolfgang* / CD / 1992 / Des: In-house / Ph: Bernard Oglesby

The Adventure Babies were the last band to sign to Factory, and Central Station Design took responsibility for their artwork. The first release, Fac 319 (see p. 202) *Camper Van*, was a hand-made three-dimensional artwork which represents 'an idyllic, idealistic, optimistic, uncorrupted 1950s lifestyle', made from card, paper, tin and lead. Art directed by Central Station Design, *Barking Mad* was photographed in one shot. It represents barking up the wrong tree.

the

adventure

babies

barking

mad

Fact 335 The Adventure Babies *Laugh* / LP / 1992 / Des: Central Station Design / Ph: Mick Green
Fac 347 The Adventure Babies *Barking Mad* / 12-inch / 1992 / Des: Central Station Design / Ph: Mick Green

The Happy Mondays recorded their final LP for Factory in Barbados. Central Station Design were inspired by naive religious icons and shrines found in countries such as this, while the image was chosen in reference to religious imagery in the lyrics. The back cover features a work of special significance to the designers since it had been painted by their sister, who had been born with Down's Syndrome. The work had been in their studio for years, and Central Station were happy to have found the opportunity to use it.

Fact 420 Happy Mondays *Yes Please!* / LP / 1992 / Des: Central Station Design

This was the final release for Factory and Happy Mondays in their original incarnation. Central Station Design return to the familiar landscape of *Delightful* (see p. 96) and *Freaky Dancin'* (see p. 105), while adopting a very different approach to the tactile qualities of *Yes Please!* (see opposite), utilizing hand-drawn and cut-out shapes which were translated through the computer, creating sprouting typographic forms. The designers also show restraint by the very subtle use of a metallic ink in the letterforms. The predominately yellow sleeve is a bookend, not only to their debut, but also to Peter Saville's Fac 1 poster.

Fac 372 Happy Mondays *Sunshine & Love* / 12-inch / 1992 / Des: Central Station Design

INDEX OF DESIGNERS

This chart gives a general overview of those responsible for the design of each item in the Factory catalogue between 1978 and 1992. Blank spaces are either unrealized projects, unallocated catalogue numbers, or items not relevant to this design survey (but which are instead listed opposite). Multi-coloured blocks represent projects that involved more than one designer or team. The chart is arranged according to 'Fac' number.

Legend:

- X — Martyn Atkins
- X — Central Station Design
- X — 8vo
- X — Mark Farrow
- X — In-house
- X — Trevor Johnson/ Johnson Panas
- X — Ben Kelly BKD
- X — Miscellaneous
- X — Peter Saville PSA

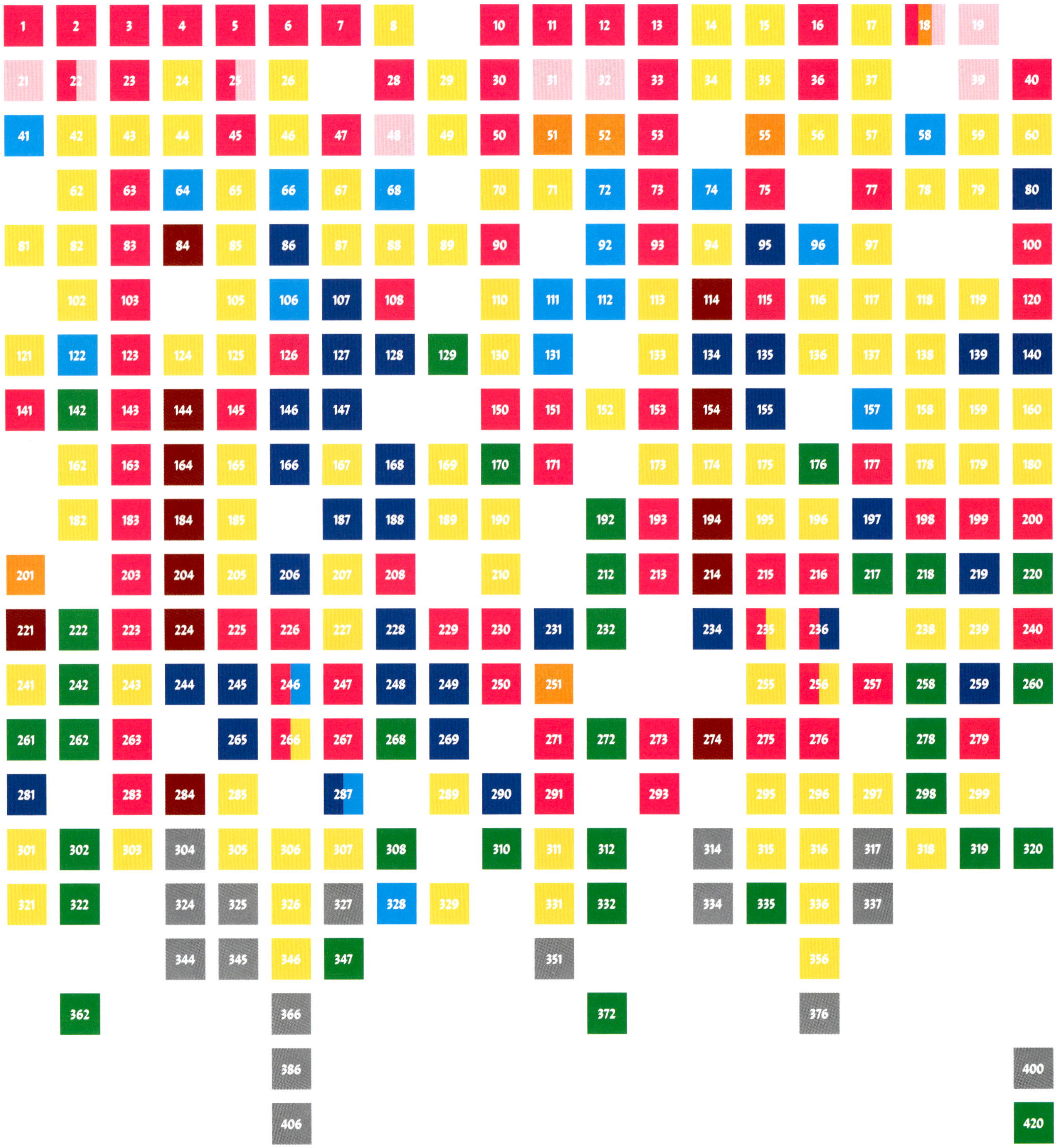

OTHER 'FAC' ITEMS

Fac 8	*Menstrual Eggtimer* / Concept / 1979
Fac 9	*Factory Flick* / Film & Event / 1979
Fac 15	*Leigh Festival, Zoo Meets Factory Halfway* / Poster & Event / 1979
Fac 20	A Certain Ratio *Too Young To Know, Too Wild To Care* / Treatment / 1981
Fac 26	*Durutti in Paris* / Poster & Event / 1980
Fac 27	*Alternative Sleeve for Fac 17* / Artwork / Unreleased
Fac 28	Joy Division *Komakino* / Flexi-disc / 1980
Fac 36	Advertising for *Closer* in USA / 1981
Fact 38	A Certain Ratio *Below the Canal* / Video / 1982
Fact 42	A Certain Ratio *The Double 12"* / 2 x 12-inch / 1982
Fac 46	*A Video Circus* / Event / 1981–4
Fac 51	*Haçienda Second Birthday* / Poster / 1984
Fac 51ʙ	New Order *Christmas at The Haçienda* / Flexi-disc / 1982
Fac 54	*Haçienda Construction* / Video / 1981
Fac 61	*FCL vs Hannett* / Lawsuit / 1982
Fac 62	A Certain Ratio *Knife Slits Water* / 12-inch / 1982
Fac 76	Jazz Defektors *The Movie* / Video / Unreleased
Fac 87	Kalima *The Smiling Hour* / 12-inch / 1983
Fac 91	*The Facsoft Computer Programme* / Concept / 1984
Fac 92	Marcel King *Reach for Love* / 12-inch / 1984
Fac 92ʀ	Marcel King *Reach for Love* / 12-inch / 1985
Fac 94	*F Dot Logo* / Badge / 1983
Fac 98	*Swing* (hairdressers) / Shop / 1983
Fac 99	*Molar Reconstruction, Rob Leo Gretton's Mouth* / Event / 1984
Fac 101	Lofts / Concept / –
Fac 104	*Madonna Inter Alia 'The Tube'* / Event / 1985
Fact 105	Biting Tongues *Feverhouse Soundtrack* / LP / 1984
Fac 108	Section 25 *Looking From a Hilltop* / 12-inch / 1984
Fac 109	Caroline Lavelle *Untitled and Undone* / Unreleased
Fac 115	*Second Generation Notepaper* / Stationery / 1984
Fac 118	52nd Street *Can't Afford (to Let You Go)* / 12-inch / 1985
Fac 121	*Riverside Exhibitions & Performances* / Poster & Event / 1984
Fact 125	*Bessy Talks Turkey* / Video / 1984
Fac 131	*It's Not Just Low-life* / Poster / 1985
Fac 132	Section 25 *Crazy Dancing* / Single / Unreleased
Fac 133	New Order *Subculture* / Single / 1985
Fac 136	*Factory Gaffer Tape* / Stationery / 1985
Fac 137	Quando Quango *Genius* / Single / 1985
Fact 137v	Various Artists *Shorts* / Video / 1985
Fac 148	*Styal Mill Bucket* / Sponsorship / –
Fac 149	The Little Big Band *First Project* / Aborted
Fac 152	*From Manchester with Love* / T-shirt / 1986
Facd 154	The Durutti Column *Circuses and Bread* / CD / 1986
Fac 156	Quando Quango *Bad Blood* / Single / Unreleased
Fac 159	*Fac Facts* / Book / 1986
Fac 161	*Out Promotion, Dave & Nicki* / Event / 1986
Fac 166	A Certain Ratio *Bootsy* / 12-inch / 1986
Fac 171	*Compact, White Columns Gallery NY* / Installation / 1986
Fact 172	The Railway Children *Singles Collection* / Concept

Fac 173	New Order *Bizarre Love Triangle* / Video / 1986
Fac 174	The Durutti Column *Valuable Press Pack* / 1986
Fac 175	*1986 Christmas Card*
Fact 177	New Order *Pumped Full of Drugs* / Video / 1986
Fact 180	*Factory Instore Tape No. 1* / Video / 1987
Fact 181	The Bailey Brothers *The Mad Fuckers* / Movie / Aborted
Fact 182	Various Artists *Salvation* / LP / 1987
Fact 186	*Festival of the Tenth Summer* / Album & Video / Unreleased
Fac 189	Miaow *Break the Code* / 7-inch / 1987
Fac 191	*The Haçienda Cat* / Feline Mammal
Fac 199	Vermorel *Bums for BPI* / Poster / 1988
Fac 202	*Dream Flight Balloons* / Sponsorship / 1987
Facd 207	The Little Big Band *Little Big Band* / CDS / 1989
Fac 208	*Disorder* / Event / 1988
Fac 209	Happy Mondays *Film Shoot* / –
Fac 211	*Wired Joy Division Feature* / Video / 1988
Fac 211	*Book of Numbers* / Concept / –
Fac 215	*Vin d'Usine Blanc* Haçienda House Wine / Bottle / –
Fac 216	*Vin d'Usine Rouge* Haçienda House Wine / Bottle / –
Facd 218	To Hell with Burgundy *Who Wants to Change the World?* / CDS / 1988
Fact 225	New Order *Substance* / Video / 1989
Fac 227	*Fred Fact* NME Feature Page / List / 1989
Fac 233	*New Order and Joy Division Accounts*
Facd 234	The Durutti Column *Womad Live* / CDS / 1989
Fac 237	New Order *Here are the Old Men* / Video Concept
Fac 238	*Haçienda '96: Citius, Altius, Fortius* / T-shirt / 1989
Fac 239	*Halcyon Daze* / Happy Mondays Fanzine / 1989
Fac 241	*Just Say No to London* / T-shirt / 1989
Fac 243	Steve Mason *Technique Cherub* / Art / 1989
Fact 244+	Vincent Gerard & Stephen Patrick *I Know Very Well How I Got My Note Wrong* / 7-inch / 1989
Fac 248	*On CD at Last, On Dat Already* / Advertisement / 1990
Facd 251	Steve and Gillian *Loved It (The New Factory)* / CDS / 1990
Fac 252	Happy Mondays *Hallelujah* / Promo CDS / 1989
Fac 253	*Chairman Resigns* / Event / 1989
Fac 254	The Durutti Column *Guitar One: House* / Demo Album / –
Fac 255	Cath Carroll *Beast* / Single / 1990
Fac 259	*Staff Christmas Party* / Event / 1990
Fac 261	*Madchester* / T-shirt / 1989
Fact 262	Happy Mondays *Madchester Rave On* / Video / 1989
Fac 264	The Durutti Column *Guitar Two: Acoustic* / Demo Album / –
Fac 265	*From Manchester with Love* / Image / 1990
Fac 270	Various Artists *Our Dance Days* / Concept
Fac 271	*Billboard Advertising for Technique* / 1989
Fac 277	Joy Division *Substance* / Video Concept
Fac 279	Revenge *Slave* / Single / 1990
Fac 280	The Wendys *More Than Enough* / Promo Single / 1990
Fac 282	*Flowers for Horse's Wedding* / Event / 1990
Fac 283	*EnglandNewOrder: Express Yourself* / T-shirt / 1990

OTHER 'FAC' ITEMS cont.

Fac 286 *Classical Showcase at Bloomsbury* / Event / 1990
Fac 288 *Shaun On One* / T-shirt Concept
Fac 289 New Order *Campaign Technique* /
Stationery / 1989
Fac 289 The Wendys *The Sun's Going to Shine for Me Soon* / Single / 1991
Fac 291 *Factory Classical Notepaper* / Stationery / 1990
Fac 292 Shaun Ryder *Colours* / Concept
Fac 294 The Durutti Column *Jazz FM Radio* /
Advertisement / 1990
Facd 296 Various Artists *Factory Classical Label* /
5 x CD / 1989
Fac 299 *Factory* / T-shirt / 1990
Fact 300 New Order / Album / Released on London
Records in 1993 (as *Republic*).
Fac 301 *Think About the Future* Factory Conference /
Event / 1990
Fac 303 Various Artists *Palatine Lane* / CD Promo / 1992
Fac 304 Various Artists *Palatine (The Single)* /
Single / 1991
Fac 305c *Select Magazine Factory Sampler* /
Cassette / 1990
Fac 306 Steve Martland *Glad Day* / Single / 1990

Fac 309 *Hi-Nek (Second Generation)* / T-shirt / Unreleased
Fac 315 Cath Carroll *Promo Package* / Art / 1991
Fac 317 Cath Carroll *England Made Me* / Badge / 1991
Fac 318 *Flying Start Exhibition Stand* / Event / 1991
Fac 321 Jonathan Demme *The Perfect Kiss* / Movie / 1985
Fac 331 Design 3 *The Temporary Contemporary* /
Boardroom Table / 1991
Fac 342 *Pills 'N' Thrills and Bellyaches* Launch /
Event / 1990
Fac 345 *Christmas Present* / Fact 400 Booklet / 1991
Fac 352 Happy Mondays *Staying Alive* / Single /
Unreleased
Fac 354 *Palatine Celebrations* / Event / –
Facd 376 Piers Adams *Handel Recorder Sonatas* / CD / 1991
Facd 386 Walter Hus *Muurwerk* / CD / 1991

FURTHER READING

Sarah Champion: *And God Created Manchester.* Manchester, 1990

Deborah Curtis: *Touching from a Distance. Ian Curtis and Joy Division.* London, 1995

Dave Haslam: *Manchester England. The Story of the Pop Cult City.* London, 1999

Mark Holt and Hamish Muir (eds.): *8vo. On the Outside.* Baden, 2005

Emily King (ed.): *Designed by Peter Saville.* London, 2003

Graham Marsh, Glyn Callingham, and Felix Cromey, (eds.): *Blue Note: The Album Cover Art.* San Francisco, 1991

Catherine McDermott (ed.): *Plans and Elevations. Ben Kelly Design.* London, 1990

Mick Middles: *From Joy Division to New Order. The True Story of Anthony H. Wilson and Factory Records.* London, 2002

Lars Muller (ed.): *ECM Sleeves of Desire: A Cover Story.* Baden, 1996

Charles Neal. *Tape Delay. Confessions from the Eighties Underground.* London, 1987

Chris Ott: *Unknown Pleasures.* New York, 2004

Rick Poynor: *Design Without Boundaries. Visual Communication in Transition.* London, 1998

Rick Poynor: *Vaughan Oliver. Visceral Pleasures.* London, 2000

Simon Reynolds: *Rip It Up and Start Again. Post-punk 1978–1984.* London, 2005

Jon Savage: *England's Dreaming. Sex Pistols and Punk Rock.* London, 1991

Jon Savage (ed.): *The Haçienda Must Be Built!.* Essex, 1992

Jon Savage: *Time Travel. From the Sex Pistols to Nirvana: Pop, Media and Sexuality, 1977–96.* London, 1997

Adrian Shaughnessy: *Sampler. Contemporary Music Graphics.* London, 1999

Nick de Ville: *Album. Style and Image in Sleeve Design.* London, 2003

Tony Wilson: *24 Hour Party People. What the Sleeve Notes Never Tell You.* London, 2002

Of the many websites dedicated to Factory and its bands, the following are particularly useful:

http://www.cerysmaticfactory.info/
http://www.factoryrecords.info
http://home.planet.nl/~frankbri/crepuscule.html

CREDITS

Artwork reproduced with the kind permission of:
Martyn Atkins pp. 28b, 30b–d, 36, 37a–b, 38b–c, 39b, 46c
Joël van Audenhaeghe p. 126b
Robert Breer p. 149a–d
Caesar / Carolyn Allen pp. 60b, 70b–c, 74a, 86d, 98c
Central Station Design pp. 96a–b, 105a–b, 115, 118, 119, 127d,
140, 141, 142–43, 144, 145, 154a–b, 155, 168a–b, 170a, 171a, 177c,
178, 179a–d, 188, 189a–c, 196a–b, 199a–b, 202b, 203, 208, 209,
214a–b, 215, 216a–b, 217
Peter Christopherson p. 39a
Alan David-Tu pp. 60a, 67a, 74c, 97a
Mark Farrow pp. 46d, 49a–b, 59a–b, 66a–b, 67b, 69a–b, 80a,
80d, 80f, 85a–b, 86c, 120a–b, 195c, 210a–b
Mark Holt / Hamish Muir pp. 81a–b, 86a, 90, 92, 95b–d,
104, 117a–b, 126a, 131a–c, 132a–c, 153a–b, 156, 175, 176, 187a–b,
194a–b, 200
David Hurren p. 202a
Trevor Johnson pp. 72a–d, 73, 80b, 80e, 82, 83a–i, 93a–b, 94,
95a, 98a, 98d, 99a–c, 103b–c, 112, 113a–b, 116b–d, 121b, 126d,
128a–c, 134f, 135a–c, 152, 157a–b, 159, 161, 163, 166, 169a–b,
174a–c, 177a–b, 180, 183c, 191, 195a–b
Mike Keane pp. 80b, 103b–c
Ben Kelly pp. 12b–c, 30a, 46b, 47a, 53c–f, 54b–c, 182
David Knopov p. 198a–b
John Macklin pp. 201b, 202c, 206a–d, 207a–e, 211,
212a–b, 213a–c
Chris Mathan pp. 77, 201a
Julian Morey p. 185
Gary Newby pp. 114c, 116a, 127c
Ann Quigley pp. 39a, 39d, 60c–d
Jon Savage p. 31b–c

Peter Saville pp. 3, 11b, 12a, 13, 16–17, 18, 19a–b, 20, 21a–b, 22,
23a–b, 24a–d, 25a–d, 27a–b, 28a–c, 29, 30a, 31a, 32a–b, 33a,
34a–b, 35, 40a–b, 41, 42, 43a–i, 44, 45, 48a–b, 51, 56b–c, 61a,
62, 63, 64, 65, 68, 71b, 75, 76, 77, 78a–b, 79a–b, 88a–b, 89,
91a–b, 97b–c, 100, 101a–b, 102a–h, 103a, 106, 107a–i, 108a–d,
109, 110a–c, 111, 121a, 122, 123, 124, 125a–c, 129a–b, 130a–b, 133,
134a–b, 136, 137, 138, 139a–b, 146, 147a–c, 148, 149e, 150a–c, 151,
157c, 164, 165, 166, 167a–d, 172a–b, 173, 181a–b, 184, 186a–c, 197
Bill Smith pp. 192a–d, 193
Slim Smith p. 114d
Colin Taylor / Michael Worthington pp. 202d, 204–205
Lawrence Weiner p. 84a–b
Ian Wright p. 38a
Malcolm Whitehead / Ikon pp. 61b–c, 71a, 71c
Tony Wilson pp. 33b–c, 71d

Photographic acknowledgments:
Tony Barratt p. 14a
Kevin Cummins p. 11a
Ben Kelly p. 15a–b
Trevor Key p. 108a–d
Carol Moss pp. 12b–c, 53c–f, 54b–c
David Murphy pp. 14b, 170–171
Julie Phipps / View Pictures pp. 160, 162a–d, 183a–b
All Trevor Key images courtesy of the Estate of Trevor Key.

*Every effort has been made to trace the copyright holders
of the images contained in this book, and we apologize
in advance for any unintentional omissions. We would be
pleased to insert the appropriate acknowledgments in any
subsequent edition of this publication.*

ACKNOWLEDGMENTS

The author would like to thank the following designers
and artists for being available for numerous discussions
and generously consenting to reproducing their work:
Martyn Atkins, Joël van Audenhaeghe, Robert Breer, Caesar
(The Wake), Central Station Design (Matt Carroll, Pat
Carroll and Karen Jackson), Peter Christopherson,
Alan David-Tu, Mark Farrow, Mark Holt and Hamish Muir,
David Hurren, Trevor Johnson, Mike Keane, Ben Kelly,
David Knopov, John Macklin, Chris Mathan, Julian Morey,
Gary Newby, Ann Quigley, Jon Savage, Peter Saville, Bill
Smith, Slim Smith, Colin Taylor, Lawrence Weiner, Malcolm
Whitehead and Brian Nicholson (Ikon), Tony Wilson,
Ian Wright

Special thanks to the following for their valuable
assistance: Rebecca Boulton, Lesley Dilcock, Andy Fisher,
Dave Haslam, Peter Hook, Daniel Mason, Martin Moscrop,
David Murphy, James Nice, Alan Parks, Mike Pickering,
Hillegonda Rietveld, Sam Rooker-Roberts, Michael
Shamberg, Howard Wakefield, Brett Wickens

And also thanks to:
Tom Atencio, Paul Barnes, Paul Cons, Jason Daley,
Michel Duval, Michael Eastwood, Jan Hargreaves /
MSIM, Mark Hindmarch, Ken Hollings, Tony Hung, Lewis
Mulatero, James Pluta, Warren Preston, Nigel Robinson,
Libby Sellers / Design Museum, Peter Shapiro, Paul Smith,
Howard Walmsley, Colin White, Marc Wood, Stephen
Wolstenholme, Jon Wozencroft, Bobby Wratten

And a personal thanks to:
Daniel & Rebecca Blackstone, Craig Bremner, Alex Brown,
Sarah Brown, John Car, Jess Carter, Jane Cutter, Christopher
Dell, Lucas Dietrich, Vincent Giarrusso, Jennie & Bill
Hindmarch, Kieron Horan, Hannah & James Reich-Levbarg,
Roger Marsh & Valerie Cooper, Tim Marshall, Kendal
Murray, Sid Newton, Tony Oliver, Sue Powell, Andrew
Robertson, Carol & Les Robertson, Ed Scotland, Gae Sharp,
Kaye Shumack, Rick Tanaka, Stephen Tredinnick, Russell &
Michelle Warren-Fisher, Anthony Wyld

Finally, the author would like to express his gratitude
to: Rick Poynor for his encouragement and guidance in
getting this project off the ground. John Cooper for his
tireless assistance in all things Factory. Nick Turner who
photographed the majority of work in this book. School
of Communication Arts, University of Western Sydney
for assistance in the preliminary stages of this project.
Tony Wilson for all his support. Kellie Hindmarch for all
her patience, effort and constant encouragement.

Introduction and captions: Matthew Robertson
Internal design and coordination: Kellie Hindmarch and
Matthew Robertson

FAC461

First paperback edition published in the United States in 2007
by Chronicle Books LLC.

First published in the United Kingdom in 2006
by Thames & Hudson Ltd., London.

Library of Congress Cataloging-in-Publication Data available.

ISBN-10: 0-8118-5642-9
ISBN-13: 978-08118-5642-3

Manufactured in China.

Distributed in Canada by Raincoast Books
9050 Shaughnessy Street
Vancouver, British Columbia V6P 6E5

10 9 8 7 6 5 4 3 2 1

Chronicle Books LLC
85 Second Street
San Francisco, California 94105

www.chroniclebooks